THE NO-LACTOSE COOKBOOK

THE NO-LACTOSE COOKBOOK

Delicious Recipes to
Satisfy Any Craving …
All Lactose Free!

Adams Media

Avon, Massachusetts

Published by
Adams Media, a division of F+W Media, Inc.
57 Littlefield Street, Avon, MA 02322. U.S.A.
www.adamsmedia.com

Contains material adapted or abridged from *The Everything® Food Allergy Cookbook* by Linda Larsen, BS, copyright © 2008 by F+W Media, Inc. ISBN 10: 1-59689-560-6, ISBN 13: 978-1-59869-560-1; and *The Everything® Lactose-Free Cookbook* by Jan McCracken, copyright © 2008 by F+W Media, Inc., ISBN 10: 1-59869-509-6, ISBN 13: 978-1-59869-509-0.

ISBN 10: 1-4405-6020-X
ISBN 13: 978-1-4405-6020-0
eISBN 10: 1-4405-6021-8
eISBN 13: 978-1-4405-6021-7

Printed in the United States of America.

10   9   8   7   6   5   4   3   2   1

Always follow safety and commonsense cooking protocol while using kitchen utensils, operating ovens and stoves, and handling uncooked food. If children are assisting in the preparation of any recipe, they should always be supervised by an adult.

This book is available at quantity discounts for bulk purchases.
For information, please call 1-800-289-0963.

Introduction

The world of lactose-free foods can be perplexing, to say the least! For people with lactose intolerance who require a low- or no-lactose diet, following this daily eating regime is crucial to preventing discomfort associated with the condition. In today's world there can be potential threats at every turn, including your own kitchen. If you are highly sensitive to lactose, each ingredient and product consumed should be scrutinized for any lactose content, which means learning to properly interpret food labels. (As a side note: many people with lactose intolerance are fine eating reasonable amounts of lactose, and don't have to be quite so strict about maintaining total compliance—for them, a little bit of cheese or dairy in a recipe will not be an issue.) To complicate matters even more, there is a long list of hidden and unfamiliar ingredients used in foods that can contain lactose even though their names may not make it obvious.

The good news is that there are plenty of tasty and healthy alternative foods and ingredients that are perfectly fine for lactose-sensitive individuals. New food options are becoming more readily available and more easily accessible every day as manufacturers realize the increased need for these products . The Internet has become an outlet to purchase specialized foods as well as a way to obtain information and support. It is extremely important to note that manufacturers often change ingredients or suppliers for their food products, so carefully reading labels on a regular basis is essential to ensuring that the foods you eat remain lactose-free. However, the process becomes easier as you learn how to interpret information and to take control of your life. *The No-Lactose Cookbook* is an easy-to-use guide to include in your arsenal of information to help make your life a little easier and a lot tastier!

Important Note: All attempts have been made in the cookbook to ensure that all recipes are totally lactose-free. However, even these foods sometimes can contain trace amounts of lactose, and many foods that we haven't included here, like some yogurt and cheeses, actually have virtually no lactose. The ingredients of any foods must be analyzed by brand to ensure they are lactose-free. All companies create different versions of different foods, so you need to check labels carefully and never assume. It is a smart idea to get in the habit of checking *all* foods, whether you know they are lactose-free or not, including those within each recipe of this book.

Happy Cooking!

Understanding Lactose-Free Diets and Cooking

chapter one

As incredible as it sounds, it's been estimated that more than 75 percent of the world's population suffers from lactose intolerance (LI) to some degree. If you find yourself in this majority category, it's important for you to take charge of your life and begin a new diet regimen that will eliminate your lactose-related discomfort, without sacrificing flavor or the enjoyment of your favorite foods! You'll be surprised how nonintrusive a smart no-lactose lifestyle can be, and the health rewards it will bring you are enormous!

What Is Lactose Intolerance?

Lactose is a primary simple sugar found in milk and dairy. In order to digest lactose, the digestive enzyme lactase must be present in the small intestine. Lactase breaks down the milk sugar into two simpler forms of sugar, glucose and galactose, which allows absorption into the bloodstream.

If there's a shortage of lactase in the small intestine, lactose carries additional fluid as it moves down to the colon. Fermentation of lactose in the colon begins to take place, and gases form. (Think of the fermentation process of champagne.) The gas bubbles can be very uncomfortable, causing gastrointestinal symptoms such as cramping flatulence, nausea, diarrhea, and abdominal bloating.

Symptoms can range from mild discomfort to severe pain, depending on each individual's degree of lactase deficiency and the amount of lactose that's been consumed. It's common for symptoms to begin anywhere from thirty minutes to three hours after eating or drinking food containing lactose.

The numbers and percentages of lactose-intolerant individuals are staggering. In fact, lactose tolerance is rarer than lactose intolerance. The National Institutes of Health report that between 80 and 100 percent of Asian Americans and Native Americans are lactose intolerant, and up to 80 percent of African Americans are lactose intolerant. On the bright side, LI is not life threatening. It can be easily controlled by diet, and it's not an all-or-nothing situation.

Medical tests can be performed with your doctor's advice to accurately diagnose lactose intolerance. It's important that you confirm the discomfort that you're experiencing after eating a meal or a snack is not a more serious digestive disorder than lactose intolerance. Consult your physician for advice on what testing needs to be done to narrow your diagnosis so that you can get on with enjoying your life.

One very simple test can be performed at home. Avoid all milk products for several consecutive days. On a weekend when you plan to be at home, don't eat any breakfast but instead drink two large glasses of milk. During the next four to five hours, if you experience LI symptoms you are a prime candidate for being lactose intolerant. At this point, see a doctor for confirmation of your symptoms.

So, What Can I Eat?

As with most things in life, there are tricks to living with LI! Because lactose intolerance is not an allergy, as one might have with gluten or soy, there are levels of discomfort you may experience that may allow you to leave some lactose in your diet.

No two cases of LI are the same. Some individuals may drink two glasses of milk without a problem, some may only be able to tolerate half a glass at a time, and some may not be able to drink milk at all! You are your own best lactose-level detective in determining your degree of tolerance for milk and dairy products. Try consuming different levels of lactose to determine how much and what foods you can eat and still feel comfortable. In general, though, you'll want to look for dairy products that are lower in lactose such as yogurt, many cheeses, and yogurt cheese, just to mention a few. In addition, there's a variety of special lactose-free milks available in the dairy case.

If your lactose intolerance is a severe case, you'll want to avoid all lactose, if possible, to maintain comfort. Instead of yogurt as a substitute, you'll want to move to silken tofu, soy yogurts, and explicitly lactose-free foods. Used in recipes, you'll never be able to tell the difference between soy and regular yogurt, but your stomach will thank you later. All of the recipes in this book make use of lactose-free ingredients, but if you feel that you have a higher tolerance for lactose, you can certainly replace some of the soy-based ingredients with low-lactose ingredients like real yogurt and cheese.

How Should I Shop for Food?

You should be able to buy most of the lactose-free food you need at any well-stocked grocery store, since you'll be avoiding a specific set of (mostly) dairy-based products. Lactose-free milk is very common now, and most national chains carry several flavors each of almond and soy milk as alternatives. Some products, like soy yogurt or soy cheese, may be slightly more specialized and require a quick trip to a health or natural foods store, but these too should be easy to locate. They're popular enough that they usually get their own section in the refrigerated aisle!

Wherever you shop, a major key to your digestive comfort is being food label–savvy. Read labels and look for the obvious lactose first. Naturally occurring lactose in milk is listed as sugar on the Nutrition Facts label on a milk carton, but the ingredients section doesn't list any added sugar. Milk is often added to some of the commercial products in the list below:

- Bread and other baked goods
- Nondairy and whipped creamers
- Drink mixes and breakfast drinks
- Margarines
- Salad dressings
- Lunch meats and hot dogs
- Processed breakfast cereals
- Candies, cookies, and snacks
- Soups (especially cream soups)
- Mixes for pancakes, biscuits, cookies, and cakes
- Sugar substitutes
- Instant coffee and cocoa mixes
- Instant mashed potatoes and French fries
- Pie crusts and pie fillings
- Pudding mixes

Not all of the products listed above contain lactose, and that's why reading labels is so important. It's important to look not only for milk and lactose among the contents, but also for such terms as whey, curds, buttermilk, malted milk, milk by-products, dry milk solids, nonfat dry milk powder, sour cream, and sweet cream, all of which contain lactose. It doesn't have to be in the dairy section to contain lactose.

Can I Live a Lactose-Free Life Happily?

Absolutely! Lactose-free food is as delicious as any other. You can still have decadent desserts, crispy fried appetizers, and hearty, stick-to-your-ribs barbecue. As long as you exercise a bit of care in your food choices, it's likely that your lactose intolerance won't hold you back at all in your culinary life. Remember, experimentation is part of the process, so don't get discouraged. When you start cooking, you may not get it right the first time. Keep trying until you do get it right.

One thing that you'll need to be cognizant of, from a nutritional perspective, is calcium. It just so happens that many of the foods LI individuals shy away from are prime sources of calcium, so keeping calcium in the diet is a primary concern for people with LI. Calcium is the primary mineral for the growth, maintenance, and repair of bones and teeth. Calcium needs to be teamed with vitamin D and phosphorus for maximum benefits. Phosphorus is important to bone structure, and vitamin D allows the absorption of calcium into the body. It's possible to have a calcium deficiency due to a lack of vitamin D; even if you are taking in enough calcium, your body can't do anything with it unless it has vitamin D.

There's a wide array of calcium-rich foods for you to choose from, and this book contains lots of recipes that are full of calcium! Here's a short list of foods that will help you make sure you're meeting your daily calcium quota:

- Dark leafy greens
- Dandelion and mustard greens
- Turnip and collard greens
- Kale
- Broccoli
- Orange juice fortified with calcium
- Whole almonds
- Sesame seeds
- Dried figs
- Blackstrap molasses
- Canned sardines and salmon with bones
- Shrimp
- Soybeans
- Beans
- Calcium-fortified soy milk
- Extra-firm tofu

For vitamin D, you can help your body out by simply taking a few minutes outside every day. As you may know, humans have the ability to absorb vitamin D from sunlight. However, your doctor may recommend that you take a vitamin D supplement if he or she feels that you may still be deficient in it. As always, make sure there is no hidden lactose in the supplement.

Lastly, be creative with your food. As long as you are meeting your basic nutritional needs, you'll never miss dairy if you challenge yourself to cook new and exciting lactose-free meals. The recipes in this book will get you started, but feel free to vary quantities, seasonings, and flavors as it suits your palate and your healthy, lactose-free life.

Good luck, and bon appetit!

Breakfast

chapter two

Breakfast Potatoes

Serves 2

1 large baking potato
1½ tablespoons margarine
¼ teaspoon celery salt
¼ teaspoon paprika
⅛ teaspoon pepper
¼ cup finely chopped fresh
   parsley

Potatoes are great for breakfast, and these will wake up your taste buds as well as your metabolism. There's no lactose in this recipe, so your tummy will be full and happy.

1. Scrub potato and pat dry. Prick several times with a fork. Place potato on paper towel in microwave oven. Microwave on high for 5–6 minutes, turning potato after 3 minutes.

2. Let potato stand for 5 minutes to cool before checking for doneness. Cut potato into ¾" cubes and set aside.

3. Place margarine in a 1½-quart casserole dish. Microwave for 30 seconds or until melted.

4. Stir celery salt, paprika, and pepper into margarine. Add potatoes and parsley. Toss all together.

5. Cover with casserole lid. Microwave on high for 2 minutes. Stir before serving.

Creamy Millet Porridge

Yes, this is the same millet you feed the birds. But buy your millet at a grocery store or food co-op, not in the pet store! This no-lactose recipe is also a superfood, and a great start to a weekday morning.

1. In a large saucepan, combine millet, apricots, and honey and stir to mix. Add nectar, water, and salt. Bring to a boil over medium-high heat, then reduce heat to low. Cover saucepan and cook for 20–30 minutes, until millet is tender.

2. Uncover saucepan and stir. Stir in tofu and serve immediately.

Serves 6

1½ cups millet
½ cup dried chopped apricots
¼ cup honey
2 cups apricot nectar
3 cups water
½ teaspoon salt
½ cup silken tofu

Scrambled Eggs

Serves 4

2 tablespoons olive oil
8 eggs
2 tablespoons water
½ teaspoon salt
Dash white pepper

Scrambled eggs are usually made with eggs beaten with milk or cream. Using water actually makes them lighter and fluffier, and it removes all the pesky lactose from the recipe so that you can enjoy this classic breakfast!

1. Heat a medium skillet over medium heat. Add olive oil. Meanwhile, combine remaining ingredients in a medium bowl and beat until frothy.

2. Add egg mixture to pan and cook, running a heatproof spatula along the bottom occasionally, until eggs form soft curds that are just set. Serve immediately.

Bacon Eggs Benedict

You can make the sauce, rice cakes, and bacon ahead of time. When you want to eat, cook the Scrambled Eggs, assemble the dish, and broil until hot. You'll never believe this cheesy, hearty breakfast dish has no lactose in it whatsoever!

1. In a medium saucepan, cook rice according to package directions for sticky rice. Cool completely. When cold, beat in egg, basil leaves, and ¼ teaspoon salt. Form mixture into 6 cakes.

2. Heat olive oil in a medium saucepan. Pan-fry cakes on both sides for 4–6 minutes per side, until golden brown. Remove from pan.

3. Cook bacon until crisp; crumble and set aside. Prepare Scrambled Eggs.

4. In a microwave-safe measuring cup, combine rice or soy milk with cornstarch or rice flour and ¼ teaspoon salt. Microwave on high for 1–2 minutes, stirring once with wire whisk during cooking time, until thick. Stir in cheese until melted.

5. Preheat broiler. Place rice cakes on a broiler pan. Top each with crumbled bacon, some of the Scrambled Eggs, and the cheese sauce. Broil 6 inches from heat source until food is hot and the tops start to brown and bubble. Serve immediately.

Serves 6

¾ cup short-grain rice
1 egg
½ teaspoon dried basil leaves
¼ teaspoon salt
1 tablespoon olive oil
4 slices bacon
1 recipe Scrambled Eggs (this chapter)
1 cup rice or soy milk
2 tablespoons cornstarch or superfine rice flour
¼ teaspoon salt
½ cup shredded, dairy-free soy cheese

Soy Cheese

Despite being lactose-free, many brands of soy cheese contain whey or casein, both dairy products, to improve mouthfeel and texture. If you are allergic to milk, you must read labels carefully to make sure no cow's milk products appear on the ingredient list. Some brands truly are dairy-free, including The Vegan Gourmet.

Spicy and Sweet Granola

Yields 12 cups; Serves 24

4 cups rolled oats
3 cups flaked rice cereal
2 cups corn flakes
½ cup sesame seeds
1 cup honey
⅓ cup vegetable oil
¼ cup orange juice
1 cup brown sugar
2 teaspoons cinnamon
1 teaspoon ground ginger
½ teaspoon ground cardamom
2 teaspoons vanilla extract
2 cups golden raisins
1 cup dried blueberries
1 cup dried cranberries

You can add or subtract spices as you'd like in this excellent breakfast cereal recipe. The oats can be omitted if you'd like; just use more corn and rice cereal.

1. Preheat oven to 300°F. In a large roasting pan, combine oats, flaked rice cereal, corn flakes, and sesame seeds and mix well.

2. In a small saucepan, combine honey, vegetable oil, orange juice, brown sugar, cinnamon, ginger, and cardamom and mix well. Heat until warm, then remove from heat and stir in vanilla. Drizzle over cereal in roasting pan and toss to coat.

3. Bake for 40–50 minutes, stirring twice, until cereals are glazed and toasted. Stir in dried fruits, then cool completely. When cool, break into pieces and store at room temperature in an airtight container.

Blueberry Pancakes

These are classic-tasting blueberry pancakes, without the dairy! Your family will never be able to tell that these are lactose-free.

1. Place flour, baking powder, baking soda, salt, and cinnamon in a sieve. Sieve into a large bowl; stir in sugar.

2. In a small bowl, combine applesauce, oil, soy milk, and orange juice and mix well. Add all at once to dry ingredients and mix just until combined; there will still be some lumps. Gently stir in blueberries and let batter stand for 10 minutes.

3. Heat a nonstick skillet over medium heat. Pour batter onto skillet in ¼-cup amounts. Cook until edges appear dry and bubbles form and just start to break on the surface. Gently turn pancakes and cook on second side until done.

Yields 12 pancakes; Serves 6

2 cups flour
1 teaspoon baking powder
1 teaspoon baking soda
¼ teaspoon salt
½ teaspoon cinnamon
⅓ cup sugar
¼ cup applesauce
2 tablespoons vegetable oil
1¼ cups soy milk
¼ cup orange juice
1½ cups blueberries

Crisp Brown-Sugar Waffles

Serves 4

1 cup superfine rice flour
½ cup millet flour
3 tablespoons brown sugar
1½ teaspoons baking powder
½ teaspoon baking soda
½ teaspoon xanthan gum
¼ teaspoon salt
1 large egg, beaten
½ cup apple juice
2 tablespoons vegetable oil
Nonstick cooking spray, as
     needed

The brown sugar caramelizes when the waffles cook, adding an extra layer of flavor to these delicious waffles.

1. Combine rice flour, millet flour, brown sugar, baking powder, baking soda, xanthan gum, and salt in a large bowl; mix with wire whisk until blended.

2. In a small bowl, combine egg, apple juice, and oil; mix well. Stir into flour mixture and mix well; let stand for 10 minutes.

3. Preheat waffle iron and spray with cooking spray. Pour batter by scant ⅓-cup measures onto heated iron, close, and cook until steaming stops. Serve waffles immediately.

Scroddled Eggs

Scroddled eggs are just barely mixed, so the white and yellow portions are still visible in the finished product. It's another take on lactose-free eggs that's a classic diner favorite.

1. Place eggs in a medium bowl. Beat with a fork just until yolks are broken and mixture is slightly frothy. Do not beat until the yolks and whites are combined.

2. Heat a medium nonstick skillet over medium heat. Add oil and swirl around pan. Pour in eggs and sprinkle with salt and pepper. Cook, shaking pan occasionally and running a heatproof spatula around the edges of the eggs, until set.

3. Carefully turn eggs with a large spatula and cook until second side is set. Eggs should be visibly white and yellow. Cut into quarters to serve.

Scroddled Eggs

Back in the Great Depression, customers at diners would ask for "scroddled" eggs because they couldn't be made with powdered egg. The white and yellow color of the partially beaten eggs can't be imitated by anything other than fresh eggs, unlike traditional scrambled eggs or omelets.

Serves 4

8 eggs
1 tablespoon olive or
   vegetable oil
½ teaspoon salt
⅛ teaspoon pepper

Multigrain Pancakes

Serves 6

1 cup whole wheat flour
½ cup all-purpose flour
¼ cup rye flour
¼ cup cornmeal
1 teaspoon baking powder
¼ cup brown sugar
½ teaspoon salt
1 teaspoon cinnamon
2 teaspoons vanilla
1 ripe banana
½ cup soy or rice milk
½ cup orange juice
½ cup apple juice
Vegetable oil, as needed

You can omit the soy or rice milk in this recipe and increase the orange and apple juices, if you'd like, without adding any lactose to the recipe. The consistency will be a bit thinner, but many people find that orange juice complements the taste of pancakes perfectly.

1. In a large bowl, combine flours, cornmeal, baking powder, brown sugar, salt, and cinnamon and mix well with wire whisk.

2. In a blender or food processor, combine vanilla, banana, and soy or rice milk; blend until smooth. Add orange and apple juices; blend until smooth again.

3. Add all at once to dry ingredients; mix with wire whisk until blended. Let batter stand for 15 minutes.

4. Heat a large nonstick skillet over medium heat. Brush oil over surface. Pour batter onto skillet, ¼ cup at a time. Cook until edges appear dry and bubbles form and just start to break on the surface. Gently turn pancakes and cook on second side until done.

Fruity Waffles

Bananas, orange juice, and blueberries combine to make an excellent, crisp waffle perfect for a luxurious breakfast.

1. In a large bowl, combine flours, sugar, baking powder, baking soda, cinnamon, and salt and mix well with wire whisk.

2. In a blender or food processor, combine bananas and rice milk; blend or process until smooth. Add orange juice and vegetable oil and blend or process until smooth.

3. Add all at once to dry ingredients and mix until just combined. Fold in blueberries.

4. Preheat the waffle iron according to directions and make waffles; brush waffle iron with a bit of vegetable oil before making first waffle.

Making Waffles

Follow the directions that come with your waffle iron to make the best waffles. Generally, you preheat the iron, grease it a bit, add the batter, close the iron, and cook until the steaming stops. The first waffle almost always sticks; after that, you should be able to turn out perfect waffles.

Yields 12 waffles; Serves 6

1 cup all-purpose flour
½ cup whole wheat flour
½ cup superfine rice flour
¼ cup granulated sugar
1½ teaspoons baking powder
1½ teaspoons baking soda
1 teaspoon cinnamon
¼ teaspoon salt
2 ripe bananas
1 cup rice milk
½ cup orange juice
2 tablespoons vegetable oil
1½ cups blueberries
Vegetable oil, as needed

Ham Omelet

Serves 4

2 tablespoons vegetable oil
½ cup chopped onion
1 cup chopped ham
1 (8-ounce) can pineapple
  tidbits
9 eggs
½ teaspoon salt
⅛ teaspoon pepper
1 cup shredded dairy-free soy
  cheese

The pineapple liquid adds a bit of sweetness to the eggs, which complements the salty ham beautifully. Make sure you're careful when purchasing your soy cheese. Most brands should be lactose-free by definition, but it never hurts to look.

1. In a large saucepan, heat vegetable oil over medium heat. Add onion and ham; cook and stir for 4–5 minutes, or until onion is crisp-tender. Remove ham and onions from skillet and set aside.

2. Drain pineapple, reserving liquid. In a medium bowl, combine 2 tablespoons reserved pineapple liquid, eggs, salt, and pepper; beat until frothy.

3. Add to hot saucepan; cook over medium heat, lifting egg mixture occasionally to let uncooked egg flow underneath. When top is set but still moist, add ham, onion, and drained pineapple.

4. Cover and cook for 2 minutes, then top with cheese. Fold omelet in half and slide onto serving plate. Serve immediately.

Egg and Veggie Scramble

Use your favorite vegetables in this easy breakfast recipe. Grating soy cheese before cooking with it helps it melt more fully and replicate the texture of traditional dairy.

1. In a large skillet, heat olive oil over medium heat. Add onion, mushrooms, and red bell pepper; cook and stir for 4–5 minutes, or until vegetables are tender. Sprinkle with salt, pepper, and thyme leaves.

2. Meanwhile, in a medium bowl combine eggs and water and beat until frothy. Add to skillet when vegetables are tender. Cook, stirring occasionally, until eggs are just set but still moist.

3. Sprinkle with cheese, remove from heat, and cover. Let stand for 3–4 minutes, or until cheese melts. Serve immediately.

Serves 4

2 tablespoons olive oil
½ cup chopped onion
1 cup sliced mushrooms
½ cup chopped red bell pepper
¼ teaspoon salt
⅛ teaspoon pepper
½ teaspoon dried thyme leaves
8 eggs
2 tablespoons water
½ cup grated, dairy-free soy cheese

Creamy Oatmeal

Serves 6

2 cups water
2 cups applesauce
1½ teaspoons cinnamon
¼ cup brown sugar
2 tablespoons honey
½ teaspoon salt
2 cups quick-cooking oatmeal
½ cup dried currants

Applesauce adds creamy texture and nutrition to this simple oatmeal recipe. It is an ideal thickener in the place of milk or cream. Serve it hot with some warmed maple syrup or honey.

1. In a large saucepan, combine water, applesauce, cinnamon, brown sugar, honey, and salt and bring to a boil.

2. Stir in oatmeal and cook for 2–4 minutes, or until mixture thickens. Stir in currants, cover, and remove from heat. Let stand for 5 minutes. Stir and serve immediately.

Buckwheat Pancakes

This variation on an old-fashioned favorite is made with buckwheat flour and tofu. You won't be able to taste the tofu, but it adds a great texture.

1. In a large mixing bowl, combine buckwheat flour, white flour, baking powder, baking soda, and salt.

2. In a blender, combine tofu, water, oil, and honey. Blend together until mixture reaches a smooth consistency. Make a well in dry ingredients and pour in contents from blender. Stir until ingredients are just combined; there will be lumps, but don't worry about them.

3. Heat a griddle or large skillet over medium-high heat. Lightly oil the skillet. Pour ¼ cup batter onto griddle for each pancake.

4. The tops of the pancakes will bubble and begin to look dry when it's time to flip them over. Flip and brown the other side for 2 minutes or until golden.

5. Serve hot with warm syrup, your favorite fruit sauce, or fruit preserves.

Stack 'Em

A pancake stack makes a deliciously edible centerpiece for a brunch or special breakfast. Place a large hot pancake on a warm serving dish and spread generously with your choice of filling. Repeat, using 4 or 5 pancakes. Top with fruit sauce that will run down the sides, fresh blueberries, and a large dollop of non-dairy whipped topping.

Yields 12 pancakes

1 cup buckwheat flour
1 cup unbleached white flour
2 teaspoons baking powder
1 teaspoon baking soda
½ teaspoon salt
½ pound soft tofu
2½ cups water
2 tablespoons oil
2 tablespoons honey
Vegetable oil, as needed

Cocoa Pancakes

Serves 6

1½ cups whole wheat pastry flour
½ cup unsweetened cocoa powder
2 tablespoons granulated sugar
1 teaspoon baking powder
½ teaspoon baking soda
½ teaspoon salt
2 cups chocolate soy milk
1 tablespoon vegetable oil
1½ teaspoons vanilla extract
½ cup carob chips
Cooking spray, as needed

Who said that you can't satisfy your chocolate craving without suffering with your LI! If you're not a fan of carob chips, there are some decadent chocolate chips on the market that are lactose-free, so do your homework if you want the real thing!

1. Sift flour, cocoa, sugar, baking powder, baking soda, and salt into a mixing bowl. Add chocolate soy milk and oil, whisking until just combined. Stir in vanilla extract. Let batter sit for 5 minutes before cooking.

2. Spray a large nonstick skillet with cooking spray. Heat skillet over medium heat. Pour ¼ cup batter on skillet for each pancake. Sprinkle pancakes with carob chips if desired.

3. Cook for 2 minutes, turning when tops begin to bubble and edges begin looking dry. Cook for 2 minutes more and remove from skillet, placing on a warm plate. Serve with syrup or yogurt and fresh fruit.

Cocoa and Antioxidants

The word cocoa doesn't necessarily bring healthy thoughts to mind. However, the fact is that one tablespoon of cocoa powder contains as many antioxidants as ⅔ cup of fresh blueberries. Cocoa contains more antioxidants than green tea and red wine!

Tart Apricot Syrup

Shock your taste buds with this tart syrup! It's a perfect accompaniment to a stack of lactose-free pancakes to start off your morning right.

1. Combine chopped dried apricots and 1 cup water in a small saucepan. Bring to a boil, cover, and simmer for 20 minutes.

2. Allow to cool. Whip contents in a blender. Add 1½ cups water or enough to reach syrup consistency.

3. Store in refrigerator.

Yields 3 cups

1 cup chopped dried apricots
2½ cups water

Blueberry Syrup

¼ cup granulated sugar
1 tablespoon plus 1½ tea-
    spoons cornstarch
1¼ cups boiling water
1 (16-ounce) package frozen
    unsweetened blueberries,
    thawed and drained
1 tablespoon lemon juice

Venture away from the usual maple syrup with this easy homemade blueberry syrup.

1. Combine sugar and cornstarch in a saucepan. Stir in boiling water. Cook over medium heat until mixture comes to a full boil, stirring constantly.

2. Reduce heat and simmer for 1 minute, stirring constantly. Remove from heat. Fold in blueberries and lemon juice.

3. Serve warm or chilled.

Fruit . . . Naturally

Fruit is naturally sweet. When you're making syrups and sauces, try to use fresh fruit whenever possible. Frozen unsweetened fruit or canned fruit packed in its own juice are good runners-up. All of these options help reduce the intake of both sugar and calories.

Pineapple Syrup

This is a very sweet syrup that your sweet tooth is sure to love. Watching calories is always important, so make a little go a long way!

Yields 2½ cups

1 cup dried pineapple
2 cups water

1. Combine the dried pineapple with 1 cup water in a small saucepan. Bring to a boil and simmer, covered, for 20 minutes. Remove from heat and cool.

2. Whip contents in a blender and add 1 cup water. Blend to syrup consistency. Add more water sparingly, until desired syrup consistency is reached.

3. Store covered in refrigerator.

Strawberry Sauce

Yields 1⅓ cups

3 cups fresh strawberries, halved
2 tablespoons orange juice concentrate
1 tablespoon granulated sugar
1 teaspoon grated orange rind
½ teaspoon grated lemon rind

Strawberries are a favorite, so spread this sauce around! This sauce has it all—great taste and lots of vitamin C and folic acid.

1. Place all ingredients in a blender. Process until smooth, scraping sides as necessary.

2. Pour mixture into a small bowl. Cover and thoroughly chill.

Fresh!

This recipe is very versatile. Spooned over waffles with a dollop of yogurt and topped with a whole fresh strawberry, it turns an everyday waffle into an LI celebration with zero grams of lactose. This same fresh sauce is great on meringues and as a dip for other fruits.

Smoothies
and Juices

chapter three

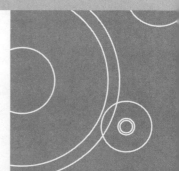

Passion Fruit Smoothie

Serves 4

½ cup plain soy yogurt
Pulp of 2 passion fruits
2 bananas
6 strawberries
⅓ cup frozen raspberries
1 cup apple juice
2 ice cubes

If you have a passion for smoothies, this one will make you smile—and it's pretty to serve, too! Soy yogurt is one of the ultimate no-lactose foods—it has many of the same benefits as yogurt, but without any risk of trace amounts of lactose remaining.

1. Place all ingredients in a blender.

2. Blend until mixture reaches a smooth consistency and serve at once.

Peachy Breakfast Nog

Oh, this one is just peachy keen! Smoothies and nogs are a great way to kick-start the day, and this one gives you a jump on your daily calcium requirement!

1. Combine all ingredients in a blender. Process until smooth.

2. Pour into glasses and serve immediately.

Lactose-Friendly Yogurt

Make your smoothies and nogs tasty, full-bodied, and healthy by adding some soy yogurt. Delicious eaten on its own as a meal or a snack, soy yogurt also makes a tasty topping for fresh fruits, works great in sauces, is a wonderful baking ingredient, makes a yummy addition to soups and casseroles, and transforms into delicious dressings and dips.

Serves 4

1½ cups peach nectar, chilled
2 (16-ounce) cans peach slices in juice, drained
1 (8-ounce) carton vanilla soy yogurt
⅛ teaspoon almond or vanilla extract

Chai Smoothie

Serves 1

1 cup soy milk
1 banana, cut in chunks
½ teaspoon ground cinnamon
⅛ teaspoon ground carda-
   mom
⅛ teaspoon ground coriander
⅛ teaspoon ground cloves
⅛ teaspoon ground black
   pepper
1 tablespoon honey
6 ice cubes

If you're a fan of Chai tea, you're gonna love this smoothie! It can be a great treat or mid-day pick-me-up. You don't have to worry about dairy in this recipe because it's made specifically with LI in mind—hence the soy milk!

1. Pour the soy milk into a blender. Add banana, cinnamon, cardamom, coriander, cloves, black pepper, honey, and ice.

2. Blend on high speed until smooth.

3. Serve immediately with fruit garnish, if desired.

Frozen Tea Ice Cubes

If you want to add to the flavor of the Chai in this smoothie, prepare Chai tea and freeze it in ice cube trays. Use the Chai cubes in place of regular ice cubes in this smoothie so as not to dilute the great Chai flavor!

Blueberry Banana Nog

The apple and the apple juice in this nog add a bit of natural sweetness to this purple-hued nog. Not peeling the apple keeps in those all-important nutrients that your body will make such good use of!

Serves 4

2 bananas
½ cup frozen blueberries
1 cored, unpeeled red apple
1¼ cups apple juice
2 ice cubes

1. Combine all ingredients in a blender. Blend until smooth.

2. Pour into serving glasses and serve immediately.

Frozen Bananas

Ripe bananas are perfect for blending. Before they get too old, peel them, put them into a resealable plastic bag, and pop them in the freezer. Frozen bananas are perfect for nogs and smoothies. If you use a frozen banana you won't need ice cubes, which dilute the flavor. Also, you'll find you don't waste bananas if you freeze them!

Kiwi Starter

Serves 4

3 sliced kiwi fruit
1 cup fresh pineapple chunks
1 banana
1 cup tropical fruit juice
2 ice cubes

If you don't have fresh pineapple, you can substitute drained, canned pineapple chunks in this recipe. The flavor will still be yummy, but fresh is always best.

1. Combine all ingredients in a blender. Blend until smooth.

2. Pour into glasses and serve immediately.

Almond Peach Nog

This is not only delicious but is also a beautiful peachy-colored drink. Some folks with LI like the taste of almond milk better than soy milk—you make the call!

1. Pour almond milk into a blender. Add peaches, honey, and vanilla and almond extracts and top with ice.

2. Blend on high speed until smooth.

3. Serve with a fresh peach slice perched on the side of the glass.

Beta-Carotene Points

Peaches are a great source of beta-carotene, which is a carotenoid that converts to vitamin A. By changing to vitamin A, beta-carotene is a high performer in your overall health. As an antioxidant vitamin, it provides protection from disease and the degenerative aspects of aging.

Serves 1

1 cup almond milk
2 large ripe peaches, peeled, pitted, and diced
1 tablespoon honey or to taste
1 teaspoon pure vanilla extract
½ teaspoon pure almond extract
6 ice cubes
Fresh peach slices for garnish (optional)

Berry Jumble Smoothie

Serves 2

½ cup soy milk
½ cup plain soy yogurt
½ cup frozen blueberries
½ cup frozen raspberries
½ cup frozen blackberries
1 frozen banana, cut in chunks
Orange slices for garnish
   (optional)

Fresh berries can always be substituted for frozen; however, you may actually prefer frozen berries. They make the smoothie thicker. Despite not having any lactose, this smoothie is packed with calcium and will really benefit your bones!

1. Pour soy milk into a blender. Add yogurt, berries, and banana.

2. Blend on high speed until smooth.

3. Garnish with orange slices as desired and serve immediately.

Deluxe Daybreak Smoothie

This breakfast smoothie makes you feel like you're pampering yourself when it's actually packed with a ton of stuff that's really good for you!

1. Blend all ingredients together in a blender until smooth.

2. Pour into glasses and serve with a spoon.

Breaking the Fast with Breakfast

Do your body and mind a big favor and don't skip breakfast—ever! Replenishing your body's blood sugar stores in the morning will help you sustain not only your physical activities throughout the day but also the mental work that you need to perform. It also improves concentration!

Serves 4

½ mango, cut in chunks
2 tablespoons oat bran
2 cups soy milk
2 tablespoons honey
¼ cup soy yogurt

Pear Nog

Serves 2

2 cups chilled pear nectar
1 (8-ounce) carton plain soy
   yogurt
¼ teaspoon almond extract

Nogs are so versatile that you can use any of your favorite juices, nectars, or fruits. This one is just for you pear lovers!

1. Combine all ingredients in a blender.

2. Process for about 30 seconds or until smooth. Serve immediately.

Nutty Straw-Nana Nog

This is a creamy and delicious nog that will even satisfy your sweet tooth. How can something so good for you also be loaded with lots of protein, minerals, and vitamins—but zero lactose?

1. Combine all ingredients except whole strawberries in a blender. Blend on high for 30 seconds.

2. Garnish with a whole strawberry if desired and serve immediately.

Serves 2

1 banana
1 cup soy milk
1 cup orange juice
10 strawberries, sliced
4 teaspoons natural peanut butter
Whole strawberries for garnish (optional)

Peanut Butter Banana Flip

Serves 2

1 cup soy milk
2 tablespoons natural peanut
  butter
1 teaspoon pure vanilla extract
1 frozen banana, cut into
  chunks
6 ice cubes

Small kids, medium kids, big kids, and adults love peanut butter and bananas together. Here's a great-tasting and energizing smoothie for a snack or a morning boost. And this one has zero tolerance for lactose!

1. Pour soy milk into a blender. Add peanut butter, vanilla, banana, and ice cubes.

2. Blend on high speed until smooth and serve immediately.

Read Those Labels!

Read the labels on those peanut butter jars to see how much salt or sugar has been added to enhance the flavor—and diminish the nutritional value!

Banana Fig Nog

Variety is the spice of life—and that includes a variety of fruits. There are so many ways for you to have a lip-smacking variety of recipes that don't aggravate your LI!

1. Pour the soy milk into a blender. Add figs, banana, cashews, vanilla, nutmeg, and ice cubes.

2. Blend until smooth and serve immediately.

Serves 3

1 cup soy milk
6 fresh ripe small black figs, cut in half
1 medium frozen banana, cut in chunks
3 tablespoons roasted cashews
1 teaspoon pure vanilla extract
½ teaspoon ground nutmeg
4–6 ice cubes

Orange Coconut Dreamsicle-in-a-Glass

Serves 3

2 oranges, peeled, cut into chunks
1 cup soy milk
½ cup grated coconut
2 teaspoons pure vanilla extract
2 teaspoons honey
6 ice cubes

If you want to enhance the delight of this delectable Dreamsicle-in-a-Glass, freeze some orange juice ice cubes ahead of time. Use the juice ice cubes in place of the plain ones. And remember when you're buying orange juice to look for the calcium-fortified variety.

1. Place orange chunks into a blender and blend on high to break up. Add milk and blend oranges and milk together just until combined.

2. Add coconut, vanilla, honey, and ice cubes.

3. Blend on high speed until smooth. Serve immediately.

Beyond Bones and Teeth

Calcium is crucial to building strong bones and teeth, but it's responsible for so much more. It helps your blood clot, your heart keep beating, and your nervous system send messages. Unfortunately, being LI makes it a challenge to get as much calcium as your body needs. Smoothies and nogs are the perfect way to combat this shortage.

Tropical Soy Nog

Be sure to peel your papaya before you cut it into chunks and throw it in the blender—the skin isn't edible!

1. Pour soy milk into a blender. Add peeled papaya, lemon zest, and vanilla. Blend on high speed until smooth and serve immediately.

Papaya Trivia

Papayas can grow to weigh up to 20 pounds! Now that's some fruit. It's deliciously tart, yet its sweet flavor complements many dishes. The papaya is a great addition to tossed salads, and you can use it as a base in refreshing smoothies for breakfast or an energy drink.

Serves 1

¾ cup soy milk
1½ cups papaya, cut in chunks and frozen
1½ teaspoons fresh lemon zest
1 teaspoon pure vanilla extract

Fruity Yogurt Smoothie

Serves 2

1 cup orange juice
1 cup fruit-flavored soy yogurt
1 frozen banana
4 ice cubes

Why not experiment with frozen tea ice cubes? Just make your favorite flavored tea and make it into ice cubes—it will add flavor to your LI-healthy and calcium-fortified smoothie!

1. Combine all ingredients in a blender.

2. Mix well until smooth. Serve immediately.

Quick Breads and Muffins

chapter four

Nutty Bran Bread

Yields 2 loaves

2 tablespoons yeast
1½ cups warm water
4 tablespoons olive oil
1 tablespoon blackstrap
   molasses
½ cup soy milk
4 cups unbleached white flour
1 cup whole wheat flour
1 cup bran cereal
1 tablespoon granulated sugar
1 tablespoon salt
½ cup walnuts

Blackstrap molasses gives the bread a noticeable sweetness and increases the nutrition—specifically the calcium—at the same time.

1. Preheat oven to 400°F.

2. Dissolve yeast in warm water. Add olive oil, molasses, and soy milk, mixing well.

3. Combine dry ingredients and chopped walnuts. Add molasses mixture and knead for at least 20 minutes.

4. Round up dough in greased bowl. Let dough rise in a warm place until doubled in size. Punch down and divide into 2 loaves.

5. Flatten dough and roll up into loaf shapes. Place in loaf pans. Let rise until doubled. Bake for 30 minutes.

Whole Wheat Flour

Whole wheat flour is natural and made from whole wheat. It isn't bleached and retains its golden brown color. Unlike other processed flours, whole wheat flour contains all the wheat germ and bran of the original grain. A heavy flour, it can be lightened by simply whisking it or sifting it.

Whole Wheat Banana Bread

This recipe adds a bit of a healthy crunch to a long-time favorite. It's a tasty breakfast on the run with some fresh fruit, and a snack to look forward to. This particular recipe is lactose friendly and a real energy booster!

1. Preheat oven to 350°F.

2. In a large bowl combine flour, wheat germ, baking soda, and salt. Make a well in center of mixture.

3. Combine banana, oil, honey, eggs, and vanilla. Add to dry ingredients. Stir together until just moistened.

4. Coat a 9" × 5" × 3" loaf pan with cooking spray. Spoon batter into pan. Bake for 60 minutes or until a wooden pick inserted in center comes out clean.

Yields 1 loaf

2 cups whole wheat flour
¼ cup wheat germ
1 teaspoon baking soda
½ teaspoon salt
1½ cups mashed ripe banana
¼ cup vegetable oil
¼ cup honey
2 eggs
1 teaspoon vanilla extract
Nonstick cooking spray

Oatmeal Poppy Seed Bread

Yields 2 loaves

1 cup plus 3 tablespoons
    rolled oats
¼ cup molasses
¼ cup margarine
2 teaspoons salt
1½ cups water
1 tablespoon poppy seeds
1 package dry yeast
¼ cup warm water
3 cups whole wheat flour
1¼ cups all-purpose flour

This is a delicious and nutritious bread that makes a great healthy snack with an extra treat of poppy seeds tucked in!

1. Preheat oven to 375°F. Grease a large baking sheet with sides and sprinkle lightly with 1 tablespoon oats. Set aside.

2. Using a large, heavy-bottomed pan, combine molasses, margarine, salt, and water and bring to a boil. Combine 1 cup oats and poppy seeds in a heat-proof bowl. Pour boiling mixture over oats and poppy seeds. Let cool to room temperature, stirring occasionally. Dissolve the yeast in the warm water and add to the oat mixture when cool.

3. Combine flours and add to oat mixture. Turn onto a floured board and knead vigorously for 6–8 minutes. Place in a greased bowl, cover, and let rise in a warm place until doubled in volume, about 60 minutes. Turn out onto a lightly floured surface. Knead dough well. Divide into 2 equal pieces.

4. Shape bread into long, pointed ovals. Place on prepared baking sheet. Chop 2 tablespoons of oats and sprinkle over the tops of the loaves. Cover loosely with waxed paper and set aside to let rise again, just short of doubling.

5. Slash each loaf diagonally 4 times with a very sharp knife. Bake for 45 minutes. The oatmeal on top will be crispy and browned.

Irish Soda Bread

This bread is best if you eat the whole thing the day that it is made! It doesn't store well, so make a big pot of soup to enjoy with fresh baked bread.

1. Preheat oven to 375°F. Lightly oil a baking sheet and set aside.

2. Measure soy milk in a large measuring cup. Add vinegar and set aside.

3. Combine flour, salt, baking soda, and baking powder in a large bowl. Mix until well blended. Add the milk mixture a little at a time to make a soft dough that isn't too sticky. Knead on a floured surface, just until dough is smooth, about 3 minutes. Shape dough into a round loaf.

4. Using a sharp knife, cut an "X" in the top. Place loaf on prepared baking sheet. Bake on center oven rack for about 45 minutes or until golden brown.

Yields 1 loaf

Vegetable oil, as needed
1½ cups soy milk
1½ tablespoons white vinegar
4 cups unbleached all-purpose
    flour
1½ teaspoons salt
1 teaspoon baking soda
½ teaspoon baking powder

Orange Blueberry Bread

Yields 1 loaf

Nonstick cooking spray
1 cup blueberries
1¾ cups plus 2 tablespoons whole-grain pastry flour
¼ cup cornmeal
1½ teaspoons baking powder
½ teaspoon baking soda
½ teaspoon salt
¾ cup sugar
6 tablespoons soft margarine
1 large egg
½ cup orange juice
2 tablespoons grated orange peel

The combination of grated orange peel and blueberries will wake up your taste buds for sure.

1. Preheat oven to 350°F. Coat a 9" × 5" loaf pan with cooking spray. Set aside.

2. Mix blueberries with 2 tablespoons of the flour in a small bowl. Set aside. Mix remaining 1¾ cups flour, cornmeal, baking powder, baking soda, and salt in a medium bowl. Set aside.

3. Place sugar and margarine in a large mixing bowl. Beat for 3 minutes on high with an electric mixer until light and fluffy. Add egg and beat well. Continue beating and add orange juice and orange peel. Place mixer on low speed, adding flour mixture gradually and blending well. Fold in blueberries.

4. Pour into prepared loaf pan. Bake for about 60 minutes or until wooden toothpick comes out clean when inserted in center. Cool on a wire rack for 5 minutes in pan. Remove pan and place back on wire rack to cool completely.

Whole Wheat Pastry Flour

If you haven't baked with whole wheat pastry flour, you're in for a treat! It feels almost like silk when you rub it between your fingers. It makes your home baking adventures light and airy. You may have to add a bit of unbleached white flour or regular whole wheat flour if the consistency of your dough isn't quite right.

Cranberry Muffins

Happiness is a cranberry muffin with a splash of tart apple flavor and a zing of orange zest. This LI-friendly breakfast will fill you up and make you forget all about dairy! Make sure to use rolled oats for proper texture.

Yields 12 muffins

1 cup rolled oats
1 cup soy yogurt
1 egg, lightly beaten
¾ cup brown sugar
¼ cup vegetable oil
2 teaspoons orange zest
1¼ cups unbleached white
   flour
1 teaspoon baking powder
½ teaspoon baking soda
½ teaspoon salt
1 cup cranberries
2 tablespoons sugar
1 tart apple, cored and
   chopped

1. Preheat oven to 375°F.

2. In a medium bowl, combine oats with yogurt. Add egg, brown sugar, oil, and orange zest. Stir together.

3. In another bowl, combine flour, baking powder, baking soda, and salt. Sift dry ingredients over yogurt mixture. Fold in until just combined.

4. Toss cranberries with sugar. Fold in cranberries and apples. Spoon into prepared muffin tins. Bake for 20–25 minutes.

Bran English Muffins

Yields 16 muffins

1⅔ cups soy milk
2 tablespoons margarine
½ teaspoon salt
1½ cups wheat bran flakes
  cereal
1 package dry yeast
¼ cup warm water
3½ to 4¼ cups all-purpose
  flour
Nonstick cooking spray
1 teaspoon cornmeal

Have your favorite lactose-free fruit purée ready to spread on one of these warm home-made English muffins.

1. Combine milk, margarine, and salt in a small pan. Cook over low heat until margarine melts. Add cereal, stirring well. Let cool at room temperature. Dissolve yeast in warm water in a large bowl. Allow to stand for 5 minutes. Stir lukewarm milk mixture into dissolved yeast.

2. Gradually stir in 3½ cups flour. Knead in enough remaining flour to make soft dough. Place dough in a large bowl coated with cooking spray. Cover and let rise in a warm place, free from drafts, for 60 minutes or until doubled in bulk. Turn dough onto a lightly floured surface.

3. Roll dough out to ½" thickness. Cut into rounds with a 3" biscuit cutter dipped in flour. Cover and let rest on floured surface for 30 minutes.

4. Coat an electric skillet with cooking spray. Heat at medium (350°F). Sprinkle lightly with cornmeal. Transfer muffins to skillet. Cook, partially covered, for 12 minutes. Turn and continue cooking, partially covered, for an additional 12 minutes.

5. Transfer to wire racks. Allow to completely cool. Split muffins, and toast until lightly browned. Store in an airtight container.

Breakfast Muffins

Need to grab breakfast on the run? Reach for these healthy muffins. Add more or less raisins and walnuts according to your personal preference. These pack plenty of protein without any lactose!

1. Preheat oven to 350°F. Prepare two muffin tins with paper muffin liners. Set aside.

2. Sift together all dry ingredients except oats. Set aside.

3. Beat together molasses and yogurt until smooth. Stir in dry ingredient mixture. Fold in oats, raisins, and walnuts (if desired), stirring until blended.

4. Allow to stand for 20 minutes. Spray muffin cups with cooking spray, and then fill them with batter. Bake for 45 minutes until golden brown.

Yields 24 muffins

1 cup unbleached white flour
1 cup rye flour
1 teaspoon baking powder
1 teaspoon salt
1 teaspoon baking soda
2 tablespoons sugar
¼ cup molasses
1¼ cup plain soy yogurt
1 cup rolled oats
1 cup raisins
½ cup walnuts (optional)
Nonstick cooking spray

Honey Oat Bran Muffins

Yields 12 muffins

2 cups oat bran
¼ cup packed dark brown
    sugar
1 tablespoon baking powder
½ teaspoon baking soda
1 cup plain soy yogurt
2 egg whites, slightly beaten
¼ cup honey
2 tablespoons oil
⅓ cup raisins
⅓ cup chopped walnuts

Made with oat bran, these muffins are a great breakfast-to-go and a great no-lactose treat with a cup of tea. Don't expect them to last long when you bake them. In fact, they may not even have a chance to get cold!

1. Heat oven to 425°F. Place 12 paper liners in muffin tin.

2. In a large bowl, mix oat bran, sugar, baking powder, and baking soda.

3. Add yogurt, egg whites, honey, and oil. Stir until ingredients are just moistened. Stir in raisins and nuts.

4. Spoon batter into muffin cups. Bake until golden brown, about 15 minutes.

5. Place individual muffins on a wire rack to cool.

Oat Bran Blessings

Oat bran is the outermost layer of the oat kernel. Not only is it a rich source of B complex vitamins, protein, minerals, and heart-healthy soluble fiber, it helps to lower blood cholesterol levels, possibly reducing the risk of heart attacks. It helps the body use insulin more efficiently—a huge asset in controlling diabetes.

Cinnamon Apple Muffins

Granny Smith apples are great for baking and cooking, but you can substitute any other cooking apple. Feel free to combine some whole wheat flour with your regular flour or, if you prefer, totally substitute with wheat flour!

1. Preheat oven to 350°F. Place 12 paper liners in a muffin tin. Peel, core, and dice apples. Set aside.

2. Mix flour, cornmeal, sugar, baking powder, baking soda, salt, and cinnamon in a large bowl. Using a separate bowl, gently toss diced apples in ½ cup of the flour mixture until well coated.

3. In a small bowl, whisk together yogurt, vanilla, margarine, and egg. Fold yogurt mixture into flour mixture until just moistened. Fold in apples.

4. Spoon batter into prepared muffin cups. Bake until toothpick inserted in the center comes out clean, about 25 minutes.

5. Allow to cool in pan for 5 minutes. Transfer to wire rack to finish cooling.

Yields 12 muffins

2 medium Granny Smith apples
1 cup all-purpose flour
¾ cup yellow cornmeal
½ cup white sugar
2 teaspoons baking powder
½ teaspoon baking soda
¼ teaspoon salt
½ teaspoon cinnamon
1 cup plain soy yogurt
1 teaspoon vanilla
¼ cup margarine, melted and cooled
1 egg

Apple Spice Bread

Yields 1 loaf; Serves 8

Cooking spray, as needed
1 cup superfine rice flour
½ cup millet flour
¼ cup sweet white sorghum flour
1 teaspoon xanthan gum
¼ teaspoon salt
1 teaspoon cinnamon
¼ teaspoon nutmeg
⅛ teaspoon allspice
⅛ teaspoon cardamom
1 teaspoon baking powder
½ teaspoon baking soda
1 cup brown sugar
2 eggs
2 tablespoons vegetable oil
1 teaspoon vanilla
½ cup applesauce
1 cup apple, peeled and grated
½ cup dried currants

Applesauce and fresh apple combine in this delicious recipe to make a quick bread perfect for a snack or after-school treat.

1. Preheat oven to 350°F. Spray a 9"× 5" loaf pan with nonstick cooking spray and set aside. In a large bowl, combine flours, xanthan gum, salt, cinnamon, nutmeg, allspice, cardamom, baking powder, and baking soda; mix well.

2. In a medium bowl, combine brown sugar, eggs, vegetable oil, vanilla, applesauce, apple, and currants; mix well. Stir into dry ingredients just until mixed. Pour into prepared pan.

3. Bake for 55–65 minutes, or until deep golden brown and toothpick inserted in center comes out clean. Let cool in pan for 5 minutes; remove to wire rack to cool completely.

Brown Sugar

Brown sugar can dry out quite quickly if kept in its original packaging. To make it last longer, buy a brown-sugar disc, a small pottery disc that is soaked in water. Pack the brown sugar into an airtight container and top with the disc; the brown sugar will not dry out. Make sure the cover is fastened securely and store in a cool, dark place.

Seasoned Breadsticks

You'll need a breadstick pan for this easy recipe. They can be found at baking supply stores and online.

1. Spray 12 breadstick molds with nonstick cooking spray; sprinkle with cornmeal. Prepare French Bread dough through Step 2. Spoon dough into prepared molds; let rise for about 20 minutes.

2. Preheat oven to 375°F. In a small bowl, combine basil, garlic powder, celery salt, thyme, and lemon zest. Sprinkle evenly over breadsticks.

3. Place a pan with 1 inch of water on rack below bread to create steam. Bake for 12–21 minutes, or until deep golden brown. Remove to wire rack; cool for 10 minutes. Serve warm.

Yields 12

Cooking spray, as needed
2 tablespoons cornmeal
1 recipe French Bread (this chapter)
1 teaspoon dried basil leaves
1 teaspoon garlic powder
1 teaspoon celery salt
1 teaspoon dried thyme leaves
2 teaspoons grated lemon zest

French Bread

1½ cups superfine rice flour
½ cup superfine brown-rice flour
½ cup millet flour
½ cup tapioca flour
3 tablespoons powdered, non-dairy vegan milk substitute
2 teaspoons xanthan gum
½ teaspoon salt
1¾ cups water
2 tablespoons honey
2½ teaspoons dry yeast
1 tablespoon lemon juice
3 tablespoons vegetable oil
Solid shortening
2 tablespoons cornmeal or millet flour

This bread is fabulous toasted and rubbed with garlic, then drizzled with olive oil and served with spaghetti or grilled chicken.

1. In a medium bowl, combine rice flour, brown-rice flour, millet flour, tapioca flour, milk substitute, xanthan gum, and salt; mix well. In a large bowl, combine water with honey; stir to mix. Add yeast; stir; let stand for 15 minutes.

2. Add lemon juice and oil to yeast mixture; add flour mixture and stir to combine; beat for 2 minutes. Dough should be sticky and quite soft.

3. Grease a French bread tin with solid shortening and sprinkle with cornmeal or millet flour. Spoon dough into prepared tin. Let rise for about 20 minutes.

4. Preheat oven to 375°F. Place a pan with 1 inch of water on rack below bread to create steam. Bake for 50–55 minutes, or until deep golden brown. Remove to wire rack to cool completely.

Banana Bread

This is just pure banana bread, with a wonderful flavor and smooth texture. But you could add ½ cup nuts, chocolate chips, or raisins if you'd like.

1. Preheat oven to 350°F. Spray a 9" × 5" loaf pan with nonstick cooking spray and set aside.

2. In a large bowl, combine oil, banana, sugar, brown sugar, and soy yogurt; beat until smooth. Stir in eggs one at a time; beat well after each addition.

3. Stir in the flour, baking soda, and 1 teaspoon cinnamon just until combined. Spoon batter into prepared loaf pan. In a small bowl, combine 2 tablespoons sugar and ½ teaspoon cinnamon; sprinkle over batter.

4. Bake for 50–60 minutes, or until deep golden brown and firm. Remove from pan and cool completely on wire rack. Store tightly covered at room temperature.

Yields 1 loaf; Serves 10

Cooking spray, as needed
⅓ cup vegetable oil
1½ cups mashed banana
   (about 3 bananas)
½ cup sugar
¼ cup brown sugar
1 tablespoon soy yogurt
2 eggs
2 cups flour
1 teaspoon baking soda
1 teaspoon cinnamon
2 tablespoons sugar
½ teaspoon cinnamon

Fruity Pear Citrus Bread

Yields 1 loaf; Serves 12

Cooking spray, as needed
1½ cups superfine rice flour
¼ cup millet flour
¼ cup potato-starch flour
1 teaspoon xanthan gum
½ cup sugar
2 teaspoons baking powder
1 teaspoon baking soda
¼ teaspoon salt
1 teaspoon vanilla
½ cup puréed pears
1 teaspoon grated orange zest
½ cup orange juice
¼ cup vegetable oil
3 tablespoons lemon juice
1 cup powdered sugar

Pears add moisture and flavor to this simple quick bread. You can omit the glaze if you'd like. This bread can be served as a quick, lactose-free dessert or sweet side dish at any dinner party.

1. Preheat oven to 375°F. Spray a 9" × 5" loaf pan with nonstick cooking spray and set aside.

2. In a large bowl, combine flours, xanthan gum, sugar, baking powder, baking soda, and salt; mix well.

3. In a small bowl, combine vanilla, pears, orange zest, orange juice, and vegetable oil; mix well. Add to dry ingredients and stir just until combined. Pour into prepared pan.

4. Bake for 35–40 minutes, or until bread is golden brown and firm. While bread is baking, combine lemon juice and powdered sugar in a small bowl. Drizzle half of the mixture over bread when it comes out of the oven.

5. Let bread cool for 10 minutes in pan; remove to wire rack. Drizzle with remaining half of lemon mixture; cool completely.

Storing Quick Breads

Most quick breads, that is, breads made with baking powder or soda instead of yeast, improve in texture and flavor if allowed to stand overnight at room temperature. Cool the bread completely, then either wrap in plastic wrap or place the bread in a plastic food storage bag and seal. Quick breads can also be frozen for longer storage.

Soups

chapter five

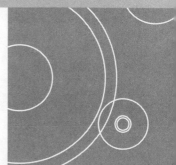

Quick Veggie Soup

Serves 4

½ pound ground chuck
¼ cup chopped green pepper
¼ cup chopped onion
1 (14-ounce) can stewed
  tomatoes, undrained
1 cup frozen mixed vegetables
1 cup water
¼ teaspoon dried whole basil
⅛ teaspoon garlic powder
½ teaspoon freshly ground
  pepper

You can cook healthfully and quickly at the same time. Use this recipe as a base and add your favorite veggies along with your favorite seasonings.

1. In a microwave-safe 2-quart casserole dish, combine ground chuck, green pepper, and chopped onion. Cover with plastic wrap. Microwave for 4 minutes on high. Stir after 2 minutes. Make sure the meat is no longer pink.

2. Drain well in a colander, patting dry with paper towels. Wipe casserole dish dry with a paper towel, returning drained meat mixture to casserole.

3. Add remaining ingredients to meat mixture. Cover with plastic wrap. Microwave for 9–10 minutes on high, stirring every 3 minutes. Serve hot.

Can You Boil Water?

If the answer is "yes," you have an unlimited world of soups to explore. Homemade soups don't have all that sodium and preservatives! Don't be afraid to change recipe ingredients—just stick with the basics and add your favorites. No worries on lactose when it comes to veggies—you've got the entire rainbow to choose from!

Zucchini Spaghetti Soup

When you're buying zucchini, look for firm, heavy fruit. For this recipe and others with zucchini, scrub the outside and slice thinly. When you peel them, you peel away a lot of nutrients, which are especially important for people with a lactose-free diet.

1. In a large saucepan, sauté onion and garlic in olive oil. Add zucchini, tomato, seasonings, and broth. Cover and simmer over low heat for 1½ hours.

2. Add short lengths of uncooked spaghetti. Continue simmering for another 10 minutes or until spaghetti is tender.

Serves 4

1 medium onion, minced
1 clove garlic, minced
¼ cup olive oil
4 medium zucchini, thinly
    sliced
1 tomato, peeled and chopped
½ teaspoon basil
Salt and pepper to taste
1 cup chicken broth
½ pound uncooked spaghetti

Cauliflower Soup

Serves 4

1 large cauliflower
6 cups water
2 tablespoons margarine
6 cubes bouillon
Salt and pepper to taste
Fresh parsley, minced
   (optional)

This creamy, smooth soup is perfect for cauliflower lovers. Who would have thought that something this "creamy" would be totally lactose-free? Serve it with a nice side salad and you're set.

1. Cut off cauliflower leaves, rinse, and cut into small pieces. Place cauliflower in a large soup pot with water, margarine, and bouillon cubes.

2. Simmer until cauliflower is tender and soft. Blend in a blender until smooth. Season to taste.

3. Sprinkle with fresh parsley and serve hot.

Split Pea Soup

Lots of people love split pea soup but have a notion that it's difficult to create. The creamy texture of this soup is sure to satisfy your yearning for dairy, and it's totally lactose-free!

1. Sort and wash dried peas. Place peas in a large heavy saucepan.

2. Add remaining ingredients. Bring to a boil. Reduce heat, cover, and simmer until peas are tender, about 1 hour.

3. Process half the mixture at a time in a blender until smooth. Serve hot.

Serves 4;
Serving size 1¼ cup

½ pound dried split peas
4 cups water
¾ cup chopped onion
½ cup chopped carrots
½ cup chopped lean ham
½ teaspoon ground celery seeds
¼ teaspoon salt
¼ teaspoon freshly ground pepper
¼ teaspoon dried whole marjoram, crushed
⅛ teaspoon dried whole thyme

Chinese Chicken Soup

Serves 4

3 boneless, skinless chicken breasts
Nonstick cooking spray
1 teaspoon olive oil
8 large fresh mushrooms, sliced
4 cups chicken broth
1 tablespoon cornstarch
2 tablespoons water
1 tablespoon soy sauce
2 tablespoons lemon juice
Lemon slices for garnish (optional)

Use this flavorful twist on chicken noodle soup to help get over a cold.

1. Cut chicken into strips. Coat a heavy medium saucepan with cooking spray. Add oil and place over medium-high heat.

2. Add chicken strips and mushrooms. Sauté, stirring occasionally. Be sure chicken is no longer pink. Add chicken broth and bring to a boil.

3. In a small bowl, combine cornstarch, water, and soy sauce. Stir until well blended, then stir into mixture in saucepan. Reduce heat and simmer for 5 minutes.

4. Remove from heat. Stir in lemon juice. Serve while hot. Garnish each bowl with a lemon slice.

Potato Leek Soup

The white and pale green sections of the leeks are the most tender and flavorful parts on this onion-like veggie.

1. Using the white and pale green part of the leek only, slice in 1"-thick pieces. Peel potatoes and cut into 2" pieces.

2. Melt margarine over medium-high heat in a large soup pot. Add the pieces of leek. Sauté until soft, not allowing to brown, about 3 minutes. Add chicken broth, potatoes, salt, and pepper. Bring to a boil. Reduce heat to low, cover, and simmer until the vegetables are fork-tender, about 20 minutes. Remove from heat.

3. Divide soup in half. Place in a blender, adding ¾ cup of soy milk. Purée until smooth. Empty soup into a large bowl. Repeat with remaining soup, adding ½ cup soy milk.

4. Place puréed soup back in soup pot. If necessary, thin the soup by adding more soy milk, a little at a time, until desired consistency is reached. Reheat soup over low heat, stirring occasionally. Take care not to boil soup. Serve hot with fresh chives for garnish if desired.

Serves 6

4 medium leeks
1½ pounds potatoes
3 tablespoons margarine
2½ cups chicken broth
½ teaspoon salt
⅛ teaspoon ground white pepper
1¼ cups soy milk
Fresh chopped chives for garnish (optional)

Pasta and Fava Bean Soup

Serves 6

1 cup fava beans
5 tablespoons olive oil
2 cloves garlic, chopped
2 large carrots, peeled and
    diced
1 large onion, cubed
2 stalks celery, diced
1 (14-ounce) can chopped
    tomatoes
7 cups chicken stock
4 tablespoons freshly chopped
    parsley
1 tablespoon freshly chopped
    oregano
½ teaspoon rosemary
½ teaspoon thyme
1 bay leaf
1¼ cups macaroni or bow tie
    pasta
Salt and pepper to taste

Dried fava beans require overnight soaking and longer cooking than canned favas. The flavor and heartiness of this soup can be attained whether you use dried fava beans or canned.

1. Soak fava beans overnight unless using canned beans. Heat oil over medium heat in a stockpot. Add garlic, carrots, onion, and celery. Sauté for 5 minutes.

2. Add chopped tomatoes, chicken stock, beans, parsley, oregano, rosemary, thyme, and bay leaf. Bring to a boil. Allow to boil rapidly for 10 minutes.

3. Reduce heat, cover, and simmer until beans are tender, about 45 minutes.

4. Add pasta and continue cooking for another 10 minutes. Pasta should be soft but not mushy. Season to taste.

Fava Bean Facts

You may hear fava beans called by other names: broad bean, English bean, horse bean, Scotch bean, Silkworm bean, and Windsor bean. You may be surprised to learn that the fava bean can be used as a coffee extender when roasted and ground!

Tortilla Soup

Tortilla soup has become a favorite in restaurants. Add more hot sauce to this easy recipe for added zing.

1. Coat a medium, heavy-bottom saucepan with cooking spray. Place over medium heat until hot. Add onion, chilies, and garlic. Cook until onion is tender, stirring frequently.

2. Add water, tomato juice, tomato, bouillon granules, cumin, chili powder, Worcestershire sauce, pepper, and hot sauce, stirring well. Bring to a boil. Reduce heat, cover, and simmer for 1 hour.

3. Cut tortillas into ½" strips. Add to soup mixture. Cover and simmer for 10 minutes.

4. Serve steaming hot. Sprinkle soy cheese over each. Garnish with a fresh cilantro sprig.

Serves 4

Nonstick cooking spray
½ cup chopped onion
1 (4-ounce) can chopped green chilies, undrained
2 cloves garlic, crushed
3¾ cups water
1½ cups tomato juice
1 medium tomato, peeled and chopped
1 teaspoon beef-flavored bouillon granules
1 teaspoon ground cumin
1 teaspoon chili powder
1 teaspoon Worcestershire sauce
¼ teaspoon pepper
3 drops hot sauce or to taste
3 (6-inch) corn tortillas
½ cup shredded soy cheese
Fresh cilantro sprigs

Cioppino

Yields 6 cups

9 littleneck clams, cleaned
½ pound fresh cod fillets
½ pound scallops
½ pound medium peeled shrimp
4 crab legs
1 medium-sized green pepper, seeded and diced
1 small onion, diced
1 clove garlic, minced
1 (16-ounce) can whole tomatoes, undrained and chopped
1 (8-ounce) can whole tomatoes, undrained and chopped
½ cup clam juice
½ cup red wine
2 tablespoons minced fresh parsley
1 tablespoon chopped fresh basil
¼ teaspoon pepper
¼ teaspoon red pepper flakes
⅛ teaspoon rubbed sage
¼ teaspoon oregano

Talk about yummy! This bouillabaisse fish stew known as cioppino is truly a seafood lover's delight. You can add squid, other types of fish, lobster—the bigger the pot, the better the stew!

1. Clean clams, cut cod fillets into 1" pieces, and cut scallops in half. Rinse shrimp and crab legs. Combine green pepper, onion, garlic, tomatoes, and clam juice in a large soup pot. Bring to a boil.

2. Add wine. Reduce heat, cover, and simmer until onion and pepper are tender, about 10 minutes. Stir in remaining ingredients. Bring to a boil. Reduce heat, cover, and simmer for another 8 minutes. Fish will flake easily and clams will open when soup is done. Be sure not to overcook. Serve hot.

More Than Just Fish Stew

The base of this delightful and fresh treat can be made ahead of time. Heat the prepared base and add the fresh seafood, which will cook in just a matter of minutes! Keep in mind that cioppino is another one of those dishes that is best when you eat the whole thing because it's not as good the next day!

Tofu Eggplant Gumbo

If you're not a tofu fan, this gumbo will ease you into it! There are so many flavors mingled in this stew that you won't even notice the tofu.

1. Cut tofu into 1" cubes. Heat ⅔ teaspoon oil in a medium nonstick sauté pan. Stir in ½ teaspoon Worcestershire sauce and celery salt. Add tofu and stir-fry until crusted and golden brown on all sides.

2. Heat remaining oil in another nonstick pan. Place onion, green onion, green peppers, celery, tomato, and eggplant in pan. Sprinkle with remaining Worcestershire sauce and spices.

3. Cook vegetables until fork-tender. Add okra and beef stock. Continue cooking until liquid thickens. Top with tofu at serving time.

Serves 4

12 ounces extra-firm tofu
1⅓ teaspoons olive oil, divided
2 teaspoons Worcestershire sauce, divided
⅛ teaspoon celery salt
½ cup onion, chopped
½ cup green onion, chopped
1¼ cups green pepper, chopped
1 cup celery, sliced
1¼ cups tomato, crushed
¾ cup eggplant, diced
2 teaspoons garlic, chopped
½ teaspoon dried thyme
⅛ teaspoon cayenne pepper
¼ cup fresh parsley, chopped
¾ cup okra, sliced
2 cups beef stock

Cold Blueberry Soup

Serves 4

1½ cups fresh blueberries
1¼ cups unsweetened grape
    juice
1 cup water
1 (3-inch) stick cinnamon
2 teaspoons sugar
1 tablespoon cornstarch
¼ cup water
¼ teaspoon ground cardamom
Extra blueberries for garnish
    (optional)

Cold fruit soups are great for a summer brunch or a special occasion.

1. Combine blueberries, grape juice, 1 cup water, cinnamon, and sugar in a medium saucepan. Bring to a boil. Reduce heat, cover, and simmer for 5 minutes.

2. Combine cornstarch and ¼ cup water. Stir until well blended. Add cardamom to cornstarch mixture. Stir mixture into soup, stirring constantly.

3. When mixture begins to thicken, remove from heat. Let cool to room temperature. Cover and refrigerate until thoroughly chilled. Remove cinnamon stick before serving. Garnish with a sprinkling of whole blueberries on top.

Cold Apricot Soup

Fresh is the word! Serve this in crystal stemmed glasses with a fresh apricot slice on the side, a shortbread cookie, and a cup of tea.

1. Combine chopped apricots, wine, and preserves in a blender. Purée until smooth.

2. Place apricot mixture in a large bowl. Add yogurt and whisk until smooth. If necessary, add soy milk to thin.

3. Cover and refrigerate for about an hour. Chill soup bowls or crystal stemmed glasses while soup is getting cold. Garnish with apricot slices.

Serves 4

3 cups fresh apricots, pitted
   and chopped
1½ cups fruity white wine
3 tablespoons apricot preserves
1 pint plain soy yogurt
Soy milk (optional)
Apricot slices for garnish

Root Vegetable Soup

Serves 6

2 tablespoons olive oil
2 onions, chopped
5 cloves garlic, minced
3 carrots, sliced
1 sweet potato, peeled and
   diced
2 potatoes, peeled and diced
2 turnips, peeled and diced
3 cups vegetable broth
2 cups water
½ teaspoon salt
⅛ teaspoon pepper
1 bay leaf
1 tablespoon fresh thyme
   leaves
⅛ teaspoon nutmeg
½ cup rice milk

Root vegetables are hearty and good for you. In this soup, they become rich and sweet as well.

1. In a large soup pot, heat olive oil over medium heat. Add onion and garlic; cook and stir for 4 minutes. Add carrots, sweet potato, potatoes, and turnips; cook and stir until glazed, about 5 minutes.

2. Add broth, water, salt, pepper, bay leaf, thyme, and nutmeg. Bring to a simmer, then reduce heat and simmer until vegetables are tender, about 20–25 minutes. Remove bay leaf.

3. Using an immersion blender, purée soup. Stir in rice milk, correct seasoning if necessary, and heat until soup steams. Serve immediately.

Creamy Beer Vegetable Chowder

This chowder should always be served with popcorn. This is a meal in itself; don't serve it as a starter!

1. In a large pot, heat olive oil over medium heat. Add onion and garlic; cook and stir until tender, about 5 minutes. Add carrots, celery, and potato; cook and stir for 5 minutes longer.

2. Add potato-starch flour, salt, and pepper; cook and stir until bubbly, about 3 minutes. Add beer; cook and stir until slightly thickened.

3. Add chicken stock and bring to a simmer. Cook, stirring occasionally, until all the vegetables are very tender, about 15–20 minutes. Using an immersion blender or potato masher, mash some of the vegetables.

4. Stir in rice milk and cheese and just heat through, stirring until cheese melts; do not boil. Serve soup topped with popcorn.

Serves 6

2 tablespoons olive oil
1 onion, diced
3 cloves garlic, minced
½ cup diced carrots
½ cup diced celery
½ cup diced, peeled potato
⅓ cup potato-starch flour
½ teaspoon salt
⅛ teaspoon white pepper
1 (12-ounce) bottle beer
3 cups chicken stock
1 cup rice milk
1 cup shredded dairy-free, vegan Cheddar cheese
2 cups popped popcorn

Ham Chowder

Serves 8

1 tablespoon olive oil
1 onion, diced
4 cloves garlic, minced
2 leeks, thinly sliced
½ teaspoon salt
⅛ teaspoon white pepper
½ teaspoon dried thyme
  leaves
2 (4-inch) fresh rosemary
  sprigs
4 potatoes, diced
2 cups baby carrots
1 cup frozen corn
2 cups cubed ham
6 cups chicken stock
1 cup water

Chowders are usually made with lots of cheese and cream. But puréeing some vegetables can create almost the same texture.

1. In a medium saucepan, heat olive oil over medium heat. Cook onion and garlic, stirring frequently, until crisp-tender, about 5 minutes. Place in a 4- to 5-quart slow cooker. Add remaining ingredients. Cover and cook on low for 8–10 hours, or until vegetables are tender.

2. Remove rosemary stems. Using a potato masher or immersion blender, mash or blend some of the vegetables in the soup, leaving others whole. Stir to blend, then serve immediately.

Tortellini Soup

This quick, satisfying soup will take the edge off your hunger on a chilly fall or winter evening. It's plenty rich to serve as a main course, even without utilizing any dairy! Make sure not to overcook the tortellini, or they can become a bit rubbery.

1. In a large soup pot, cook sausage with onion and garlic until sausage is browned, stirring to break up meat. Drain mixture. Add stock, water, salt, pepper, carrots, squash, tomatoes, basil, and marjoram. Bring to a boil, then reduce heat. Cover and simmer for 25 minutes.

2. Add tortellini and corn and bring back to a simmer. Cook until tortellini are hot and tender, about 15–20 minutes. Garnish with parsley and serve immediately.

Serves 6

½ pound ground spicy pork sausage
1 onion, chopped
3 cloves garlic, minced
4 cups chicken stock
2 cups water
½ teaspoon salt
⅛ teaspoon white pepper
1 cup baby carrots
1½ cups sliced yellow summer squash
1 (14-ounce) can diced tomatoes, undrained
½ teaspoon dried basil leaves
½ teaspoon dried marjoram leaves
1 (8-ounce) package frozen chicken tortellini
1 cup frozen corn
¼ cup chopped flat-leaf parsley

Lentil Soup

Serves 6

1 tablespoon olive oil
1 onion, chopped
2 cloves garlic, minced
3 stalks celery, chopped
2 cups lentils, sorted
1 potato, peeled and chopped
4 cups water
3 cups chicken stock
½ teaspoon dried thyme
    leaves
½ teaspoon dried marjoram
    leaves
½ teaspoon salt
⅛ teaspoon pepper

Lentils are the fast food of the legume world; they take only about 30 minutes to cook. They're divine in this silky soup.

1. In a large soup pot, heat olive oil over medium heat. Add onion, garlic, and celery; sauté for 5 minutes. Stir in lentils and potatoes; cook and stir for 1 minute longer.

2. Add water, stock, thyme, marjoram, salt, and pepper to pot and bring to a boil. Reduce heat, cover pot, and simmer for about 1 hour, until lentils are tender. Using an immersion blender or potato masher, mash some of the potatoes and lentils.

Changing Soup Recipes

Soups are probably the most tolerant of all recipes. You can add or subtract ingredients at will, and as long as you include enough water, they'll work. You can substitute beef stock or vegetable broth for chicken stock, use all water, add carrots or zucchini or chunks of ham, and it will still be wonderful.

Seafood Corn Chowder

If you use cooked, cubed ham or chicken instead of the seafood, this rich chowder can be served to those who don't enjoy seafood. Add ham or chicken at the same time you would add the fish.

1. In a large saucepan, cook bacon until crisp; drain on paper towels, crumble, and set aside. Add olive oil to bacon fat remaining in pan.

2. Cook shallots and garlic for 3 minutes, then add celery, corn, and potatoes. Cook and stir for 5 minutes.

3. Add water, salt, pepper, and oregano and bring to a boil. Reduce heat to low, cover pan, and simmer for 15–20 minutes, or until potatoes are tender. Using a potato masher, mash some of the potatoes.

4. Add fish and bring back to a simmer. Cook for 7–10 minutes, until fish is opaque. In a small bowl, combine cornstarch and rice milk. Add to soup and simmer until thickened, about 4–5 minutes. Serve immediately.

Serves 4

3 slices bacon
1 tablespoon olive oil
2 shallots, minced
2 cloves garlic, minced
2 stalks celery, chopped
2 cups frozen corn
2 potatoes, peeled and cubed
4 cups water
½ teaspoon salt
⅛ teaspoon white pepper
½ teaspoon dried oregano
1 pound cod or haddock fillets, cubed
2 tablespoons cornstarch
¼ cup rice milk

Salads

chapter six

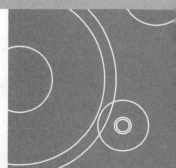

Oriental Spinach Salad

Serves 8

1 pound fresh spinach leaves, torn
2 cups shredded Chinese cabbage
½ pound fresh mushrooms, sliced
3 green onions, sliced
2 tablespoons toasted sesame seeds
2 tablespoons vinegar
2 tablespoons vegetable oil
1 tablespoon soy sauce
¼ teaspoon ground ginger

The mild flavor of Chinese cabbage combined with fresh spinach is enhanced by the ginger and soy sauce. If you have fresh ginger on hand, use it in place of the ground ginger. Its flavor is stronger and tastier.

1. In a large salad bowl, combine spinach, cabbage, mushrooms, onions, and sesame seeds. Lightly toss.

2. Combine vinegar, oil, soy sauce, and ginger in a jar with a lid; cover tightly and shake vigorously. Pour over salad.

3. Gently toss and serve immediately.

Spinach Radicchio Salad

Your taste buds will stand at attention for the radicchio in this salad. With its tender and firm texture, it has a slight bite when eaten alone; however, it adds flavor when mixed with other greens and veggies.

1. In a salad bowl, combine radicchio, spinach, mushrooms, red pepper, and olives. Chill until serving time.

2. Combine vinegar, lemon juice, olive oil, and pepper in a glass jar with lid. Make sure lid is secure and shake vigorously.

3. Pour mixture evenly over salad and toss. Distribute evenly in individual chilled salad bowls.

Serves 4

¼ pound radicchio, washed
½ pound fresh spinach, washed and torn
½ cup thinly sliced fresh mushrooms
1 sweet red pepper, seeded and thinly sliced
8 pitted ripe olives, sliced
¼ cup red wine vinegar
2 tablespoons lemon juice
1 tablespoon plus 1½ teaspoons olive oil
¼ teaspoon freshly ground pepper

Tofu Tossed Salad

Serves 6

1 bunch red leaf lettuce
1 (5-ounce) container alfalfa
  sprouts
1 small jicama, peeled and
  sliced into strips
½ dill pickle, chopped
1 tablespoon fresh chopped
  cilantro
1 (6-ounce) jar marinated
  artichoke hearts, drained
2 zucchini, sliced
2 green onions, minced
¼ pound fresh mushrooms,
  sliced
2 ripe tomatoes, sliced
1 (14-ounce) container firm
  tofu
½ cup Italian salad dressing

This salad is tossed with all kinds of tasty and healthy things. The tofu absorbs the flavors around it, and the alfalfa sprouts and jicama add crunch.

1. Tear red leaf lettuce into small pieces.

2. In a large bowl, combine lettuce, sprouts, jicama, pickle, cilantro, artichoke hearts, zucchini, green onions, mushrooms, and tomatoes.

3. Drain tofu and cut into small squares. Add to salad.

4. Pour your favorite Italian salad dressing over salad just before serving. Toss well.

Jicama Trivia

Jicama is sometimes referred to as the Mexican potato. It's key in stir-fry recipes in place of water chestnuts; it provides the same crunch! Peel jicama just before using it; like potatoes, it turns dark when exposed to the air. Jicama is an excellent source of vitamin C.

Fresh Greens and Red Pepper Dressing

Take a little extra time and go to the trouble of roasting the red peppers—you won't be sorry! If you do it once, you'll do it for many other recipes.

1. Preheat oven to 425°F. Cut pepper in half lengthwise. Remove seeds and membrane. Place pepper, skin side up, on a foil-lined baking sheet. Bake for about 20 minutes or until skin is browned.

2. Cover with aluminum foil. Set aside and allow to cool. When pepper is cooled to room temperature, peel and discard skin.

3. Blend roasted pepper, vinegar, water, olive oil, salt, and ground red pepper until smooth. Place roasted pepper mixture in a small bowl. Stir in basil. Cover tightly and refrigerate for at least 60 minutes.

4. In a large bowl, combine lettuces, tomato, and cucumber. Toss gently.

5. Top with red pepper mixture over salads and serve immediately.

Serves 6

1 large sweet red pepper
3 tablespoons white wine vinegar
2 tablespoons water
2 teaspoons olive oil
¼ teaspoon salt
⅛ teaspoon ground red pepper
1 tablespoon minced fresh basil
2 cups torn red leaf lettuce
2 cups torn green leaf lettuce
2 cups torn romaine lettuce
1 cup chopped tomato
1 cup chopped cucumber

Tofu Garden Salad with Sesame Dressing

Serves 4

¼ cup sugar
⅔ cup white wine vinegar
1 tablespoon soy sauce
1½ teaspoons sesame oil
2 teaspoons salt
Freshly ground pepper
1 cucumber, very thinly sliced
1 carrot, cut in thin strips
2 small bell peppers, cut into strips
1 large ripe tomato
1 (4-ounce) package fresh mushrooms
4 ounces bean sprouts
4 ounces whole snow peas
½ (14-ounce) cake firm tofu
3 tablespoons oil

This salad is packed with all kinds of wonderful garden veggies! If you're fortunate enough to shop farmers' markets you'll have super fresh ingredients for this gardener's delight of a salad!

1. Prepare dressing first by combining sugar, vinegar, soy sauce, sesame oil, salt, and pepper to taste. Blend well.

2. Seed and cut the tomato into ½" pieces; wash and slice the mushrooms; blanch the bean sprouts and drain well; trim the ends of the snow peas; cut tofu into ½" cubes. Cut the remaining vegetables.

3. In a heavy skillet, heat oil until hot. Sauté tofu pieces until they turn light brown at the edges (about 5 minutes). Drain well on paper towels.

4. Add tofu to vegetables. Pour dressing over all and toss lightly to coat. Serve immediately.

Papaya Salad

This is a very refreshing salad—not to mention a very pretty presentation—served in a scooped-out papaya!

1. Halve the papaya and scoop out seeds. Leave about ¼" of flesh in the shell of the papaya. Remove the rest of the flesh and dice into ½" cubes.

2. Combine the bell pepper, celery, green onion, and crab meat with the papaya. Place in refrigerator while making dressing.

3. In a small bowl, combine the yogurt, honey, orange zest, and cinnamon. Stir well to blend ingredients. Set aside.

4. Fill the papaya shell and garnish with the orange sections and sliced kiwi. Top with honey dressing. Chill before serving.

Papaya Trivia

This yellow-orange fruit contains papain, which is an enzyme similar to pepsin, the digestive juice. The seeds of papayas are usually thrown away; however, they can be dried and used like peppercorns. Papaya is very high in vitamin C and beta-carotene.

Serves 4

1 fresh papaya
1 small fresh bell pepper, chopped
2 stalks celery, diced
2 green onions, thinly sliced
1 pound fresh crab meat
1 cup plain soy yogurt
2 tablespoons honey
2 teaspoons orange zest
1 teaspoon cinnamon
1 orange, peeled and sectioned
1 kiwi fruit, peeled and sliced
Salt to taste (optional)

Cool-as-a-Cucumber Salad

Serves 4

2 cucumbers, thinly sliced
1½ tablespoons balsamic
    vinegar
½ teaspoon salt
1 tablespoon sugar
1 cup plain soy yogurt
1 green onion, snipped
½ teaspoon celery seed
¼ teaspoon dry mustard

This is a great summer supper salad. It needs to chill in the refrigerator for at least 8 hours so the flavors can mingle.

1. Slice cucumbers and place in refrigerator.

2. Combine remaining ingredients in a blender. Mix well until smooth.

3. Pour dressing over cucumbers.

4. Cover and refrigerate for several hours or overnight.

Marinated Avocado and Mushroom Salad

Be sure to let this salad happily marinate in the fridge for about 3 hours before serving so the flavors can mingle. Serve as a light summer entrée.

1. Cut avocados in half and remove pits. Peel and slice.

2. In a large bowl, combine avocado, mushrooms, and onion rings. Sprinkle lemon juice over avocado mixture to prevent avocado from turning dark.

3. In a screw-top jar, combine oil, wine, vinegar, sugar, salt, and basil. Shake well and pour over vegetables.

4. Cover salad tightly and chill for at least 3 hours, stirring occasionally.

5. Drain avocado mixture. Serve on chilled salad plates on Bibb lettuce leaves.

Serves 4

2 medium avocados
1 cup sliced fresh mushrooms
2 thin slices onion, separated in rings
2 teaspoons lemon juice
¼ cup salad oil
¼ cup dry white wine
2 tablespoons vinegar
½ teaspoon sugar
¼ teaspoon salt
¼ teaspoon dried basil, crumbled
Bibb lettuce leaves for serving

Zucchini Macaroni Salad

Serves 6

2 cups small summer squash
3 cups shell macaroni, cooked
2 cups cabbage, shredded
1 cup carrots, shredded
½ cup green pepper, chopped
½ cup red radishes, sliced
3 tablespoons onion, minced
1 cup plain soy yogurt
2 tablespoons lemon juice
1½ teaspoons sugar
1½ teaspoons dry mustard
1 teaspoon salt
Dill seed
Leaf lettuce

A little twist on other recipes for macaroni salad, this one is made with soy yogurt instead of mayonnaise for a lactose-free rendition of a summertime classic. Make sure that you allow the salad to chill for at least an hour.

1. Wash summer squash and dice but don't peel.

2. Combine all ingredients except dill seed and leaf lettuce in a large bowl. Toss to mix well.

3. Sprinkle with dill seed. Chill well, for at least 1 hour.

4. Arrange leaf lettuce on salad plates and spoon salad on top of lettuce. Serve immediately.

Zukes!

Zucchini has a mild and unobtrusive flavor and therefore is a complement to other ingredients in many recipes. It is low in calories and a good source of vitamins A and C and folate.

New Potato Salad

Off for a summer picnic? This is a great potato salad to tote along because it doesn't contain any mayonnaise. Try chilling it prior to taking it on a picnic and packing it in a cooler.

1. Scrub potatoes. Cook in salted water for 20 minutes until potatoes are tender yet still firm. Drain and cool at room temperature. Cut into bite-sized pieces.

2. In a large bowl combine potatoes, peppers, celery, onion, and herbs.

3. Combine oil, vinegar, thyme, salt, and pepper in a jar with a screw top. Shake until blended. Pour over potato mixture.

4. Toss gently until all the vegetables are thoroughly coated. Serve at room temperature.

Keep the Skins on Potatoes!

When you peel potatoes, you peel away most of the nutrients! Rather than peeling them, keep the skins on. Scrub them really well with a vegetable brush. The flavor of the potatoes is even better with their jackets left on!

Serves 10

4 pounds new potatoes
½ cup chopped red bell pepper
½ cup chopped green bell pepper
¼ cup chopped celery
¼ cup chopped red onion
¼ cup chopped chives
2 tablespoons minced parsley
¼ cup oil
2 tablespoons red wine vinegar
1 teaspoon dried thyme
Salt and pepper to taste

Strawberry Spinach Salad

Serves 6

6 cups fresh spinach
1 teaspoon toasted sesame
   seeds
2 cups fresh strawberries
¼ cup light olive oil
2 tablespoons red wine
   vinegar
1½ tablespoons sugar
1½ teaspoons minced fresh
   dill
⅛ teaspoon onion powder
⅛ teaspoon garlic powder
⅛ teaspoon dry mustard
⅛ teaspoon salt (optional)

The flavor of fresh dill and fresh strawberries together is quite an adventure for your taste buds! This salad spells summer and is great served for a special summer luncheon or supper. You can serve it as a side salad or an entrée.

1. Wash the spinach carefully. Remove stems and heavy veins. Tear into bite-sized pieces.

2. Place spinach in a large bowl. Sprinkle with the toasted sesame seeds.

3. Cut strawberries into halves or quarters. Add strawberries to the spinach.

4. In a screw-top jar, combine the remaining ingredients. Shake until well mixed. Chill.

5. Shake dressing again and pour over spinach mixture. Toss gently. Garnish with a whole strawberry, if desired.

Sweet Strawberries

Did you know that more than seventy varieties of strawberries are grown in the United States? Even though strawberry seeds may get stuck in your teeth from time to time, those seeds provide you with insoluble fiber. Strawberries are a great source of pectin and soluble fibers that research shows may help lower cholesterol.

Cauliflower Salad

You can use store-bought Italian dressing in this recipe or make your own. If you do use store-bought, don't forget to read the label and look for hidden lactose.

1. Thinly slice cauliflower; chop red pepper, and dice the celery and green onion. Combine all in a medium bowl.

2. Combine yogurt and salad dressing in a small bowl. Pour over cauliflower mixture. Toss to coat evenly.

3. Cover tightly. Refrigerate until thoroughly chilled.

4. Arrange lettuce leaves on individual salad plates. Spoon chilled vegetable mixture evenly over lettuce. Garnish with a dash of paprika, if desired.

Serves 6

3½ cups cauliflower florets
¼ cup sweet red pepper
¼ cup celery
1 tablespoon green onion
¼ cup plain soy yogurt
3 tablespoons Italian salad
    dressing
6 leaves red leaf lettuce
Paprika for garnish (optional)

Wild Rice Cranberry Salad

Serves 4

6 ounces wild rice, uncooked
6 ounces fresh cranberries
¼ cup cranberry juice cocktail
1 tablespoon sugar
½ cup carrots, cut in strips
1 cup minced green onions
1 tablespoon apple cider
   vinegar
2 teaspoons peanut oil
Dash freshly ground pepper

The vividness of this salad is second only to its incredible tastiness! Serve chilled or at room temperature.

1. Prepare rice according to package directions. Set aside.

2. Combine cranberries, juice, and sugar in a medium saucepan. Cook over medium heat. Stir occasionally until cranberries pop, about 5 minutes.

3. Remove from heat and cool slightly.

4. Transfer cranberry mixture to a large mixing bowl. Add remaining ingredients. Toss gently until combined well.

5. Cover and refrigerate until serving time.

Spinach Fruit Salad

This is a delicious fruit salad with a healthy twist. The spinach adds flavor and vital nutrients to this lactose-free meal!

1. In a food processor or blender, combine ½ cup strawberries, lemon juice, sugar, salt, mustard, minced onion, apple juice, and olive oil; process or blend until smooth. Cover and refrigerate for up to 3 days.

2. In a serving bowl, toss together spinach, watercress, 2 cups strawberries, and raspberries. Drizzle with half of the dressing; toss again. Serve immediately with remaining dressing on the side.

Serves 6

½ cup sliced strawberries
1 tablespoon lemon juice
1 tablespoon sugar
¼ teaspoon salt
1 tablespoon mustard
1 tablespoon minced onion
¼ cup apple juice
¼ cup extra-virgin olive oil
6 cups baby spinach
2 cups watercress
2 cups sliced strawberries
1 cup raspberries

Tomato Arranged Salad

Serves 4

2 red tomatoes
2 yellow tomatoes
3 plum tomatoes
1 cup grape tomatoes
¼ cup olive oil
2 tablespoons lemon juice
1 tablespoon honey
1 teaspoon curry powder
⅛ teaspoon pepper
¼ teaspoon salt

Tomatoes are so good for you, and delicious with this delicately flavored salad dressing. Serve this recipe in late summer when the fruit is at its peak.

1. Core red, yellow, and plum tomatoes and slice ½" thick. Arrange on a serving plate; top with grape tomatoes.

2. In a small bowl, combine remaining ingredients and mix with wire whisk until blended. Drizzle over tomatoes and let stand for 20 minutes, then serve.

Greens and Fruit Salad

The dressing from this salad can be used on any tossed salad. Try it the next time you make a pasta salad.

1. In a serving bowl, toss together salad greens, spinach, grapes, and orange; set aside.

2. In a small bottle with a screw-top lid, combine remaining ingredients. Seal lid and shake vigorously to blend salad dressing. Pour over the ingredients in serving bowl, toss lightly, and serve immediately.

Packaged Greens or Fresh?

For the freshest greens, pick those that have not been processed and packaged and are ready to use. There is less risk of cross-contamination, and you have control over exactly what is in your salad. Wash the greens by rinsing in cold water, then dry by rolling the leaves in a kitchen towel.

Serves 4

4 cups mixed salad greens
2 cups baby spinach leaves
2 cups red grapes
1 orange, peeled and chopped
¼ cup orange juice
2 tablespoons honey
¼ cup olive oil
1 tablespoon Dijon mustard
¼ teaspoon ground ginger
¼ teaspoon salt
⅛ teaspoon white pepper

Curried Salmon-Apple Salad

Serves 8

2 (8-ounce) salmon fillets
1 tablespoon olive oil
1 teaspoon curry powder
1 (12-ounce) box rice shell
   pasta
½ cup Italian salad dressing
2 tablespoons rice milk
2 teaspoons curry powder
¼ cup chutney
2 apples, cored and chopped
½ cup golden raisins
½ cup walnuts, toasted
6 cups mixed salad greens

Add some walnuts or pecans to this salad for a nice crunch and infusion of flavor and protein. This hearty salad is full of nutrients and will keep you going for hours!

1. Preheat broiler. Place salmon fillets on broiler pan; brush with olive oil; sprinkle with 1 teaspoon curry powder. Broil 6 inches from heat source for 8–10 minutes, or until fish flakes easily when tested with a fork. Remove from oven and let cool for 30–40 minutes.

2. Bring a large pot of water to a boil. Cook pasta according to package directions, until al dente.

3. While the pasta is cooking, combine dressing, rice milk, curry powder, and chutney in a large bowl. Drain pasta; add to dressing mixture. Flake salmon; add to pasta along with apples, raisins, and nuts; stir to coat.

4. Cover salad and refrigerate for 2–3 hours to blend flavors before serving. Serve on mixed salad greens.

Dips, Spreads, and Sauces

chapter seven

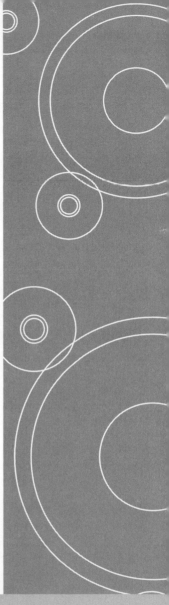

Spicy Tuna Dip

Serves 12

1 (12-ounce) can tuna, packed in water
1 (8-ounce) bottle chili sauce
3 tablespoons lemon juice
Dash Tabasco sauce
1 (7-ounce) bag corn chips

Get healthy corn chips. This dip is a great healthy snack, so don't mess it up with chips that are full of preservatives and hidden sugars! It can be used as a spread for a quick snack.

1. Drain tuna. In a small bowl, mix tuna, chili sauce, and lemon juice.

2. Add Tabasco sauce. Chill thoroughly.

3. Serve with corn chips.

Festive Spinach Dip

Even people who don't like spinach like spinach dip! Serve spinach dip with a platter of fresh vegetables or whole wheat crackers.

1. Finely chop spinach.

2. In a medium-sized bowl, combine all ingredients and mix well.

3. Cover tightly and chill for several hours before serving.

Serves 12

10 ounces frozen chopped spinach, thawed and drained
1 cup plain soy yogurt
⅓ cup margarine
¼ cup onion, chopped
2 tablespoons parsley flakes
½ teaspoon pepper
½ teaspoon rosemary leaves

Hummus Dip

Serves 6

12 ounces drained, cooked
   chickpeas
6 ounces soft tofu
¼ cup chopped onion
¼ cup chicken broth
2 tablespoons soy sauce
2 tablespoons dry white wine
1 tablespoon olive oil
1 garlic clove, minced
¼ teaspoon ground cumin
¼ teaspoon ground red pepper
3 cups assorted raw
   vegetables; carrot sticks,
   cucumber rounds, sliced
   yellow squash

There isn't a vegetable in the "veggie rainbow" that isn't good dipped in hummus! Carrots, cucumbers, and squash work particularly well, but be sure to include your favorites in this tasty and bold display of natural color and goodness. Best of all, the entire "veggie rainbow" is lactose-free!

1. Combine all ingredients except assorted vegetables in a blender. Purée until smooth.

2. Transfer to a serving bowl and surround with a rainbow of vegetables.

Recipe Variation

You can easily make this into a salad dressing by adding ¼ cup of liquid. Water is usually the liquid of choice; however, you could also use ¼ cup of your favorite wine! Hummus is also good used as a spread on whole wheat bread with some sliced turkey and trimmings.

Lemon Chive Dip

When you're preparing lemon zest, be sure to scrub the peel before zesting. Lemon trees are sometimes sprayed with fungicides and pesticides to prevent the growth of mold and to kill insects.

1. In a deep, small mixing bowl, combine yogurt, chives, lemon juice, lemon zest, salt, and freshly ground pepper.

2. Stir until well blended.

3. Chill well. Use as a dip for fresh veggies or as an accompaniment to grilled fish or chicken.

Chive Chat

Chives are of the onion clan. They are the babies of the group, being the smallest and mildest member of the family. Fresh chives are a bit on the fragile side and will wilt quickly. Use chives to enhance salads, soups, soy yogurt, and tofu.

Serves 8

1 cup plain soy yogurt
3 tablespoons chopped fresh chives
1 tablespoon fresh lemon juice
½ teaspoon finely grated lemon zest
¼ teaspoon salt
¼ teaspoon freshly ground pepper

Strawberry Yogurt Dip

Serves 6

1 cup vanilla soy yogurt
1 teaspoon finely grated lemon
  peel
1 teaspoon lemon juice
½ cup powdered sugar
2 cups fresh strawberries with
  stems

This is a cooling and delightful dessert in the summer. If you're in a hurry to serve, pop the dip in the freezer for about 10 minutes.

1. In a medium-sized mixing bowl, combine yogurt, lemon peel, lemon juice, and powdered sugar. Beat until blended well and light and fluffy.

2. Chill well.

3. Place in small serving bowls and surround with large, fresh strawberries.

Banana Peanut Butter Dip

What's better than peanut butter and bananas? Elvis had a peanut butter and banana sandwich almost every day when he was growing up! This creamy dip is bound to become a favorite for serving guests and for everyday snacking!

Serves 3

3 ounces firm tofu
1 tablespoon peanut butter
½ medium ripe banana, mashed
1 teaspoon lemon juice
1 teaspoon honey
1 teaspoon vanilla extract
2 teaspoons sugar
Ground cinnamon to taste

1. Drain tofu. Rinse and slice.

2. Place tofu between layers of paper towels to soak up excess water.

3. In a small bowl, mash tofu with a fork. Add remaining ingredients, mixing well.

4. Chill. Sprinkle with cinnamon before serving.

Peanutty Prattle!

Peanut butter made its public debut alongside ice cream cones, hot dogs, and hamburgers at the 1904 World's Fair in St. Louis. The original patent was held by Dr. John Harvey Kellogg—the same Kellogg whose name adorns cereal boxes in today's supermarkets.

Tofu Guacamole Dip

Serves 8

½ cup firm tofu
2 ripe avocados
½ small onion, minced
1 clove garlic, minced
1 tablespoon lemon juice
1 teaspoon Worcestershire
   sauce
3 drops hot pepper sauce
   (optional)
1 teaspoon salt
1 tablespoon salsa

If you like heat, then add hot salsa to this dip. If your mouth says no, then skip the pepper sauce and add a mild salsa for a smooth and mild guacamole dip.

1. Drain and rinse tofu. Pat dry with paper towels. Place tofu in a blender and blend until smooth.

2. Halve avocados; pit and peel. Mash avocados with a fork in a small bowl.

3. Add tofu and other ingredients to mashed avocados. Mix well.

4. Press a piece of plastic wrap on the surface of the dip to prevent darkening. Chill.

5. Serve as a dip for fresh vegetables, chips, or as a topping for taco salad.

Tomato Pesto

Serve this fresh tomato pesto over pasta or fresh vegetables.

1. Coarsely chop tomatoes. Seed and coarsely chop red pepper.

2. Combine tomato, red pepper, parsley, garlic, and basil in a blender. Process until finely puréed.

3. Add flour, salt, and pepper to mixture. Process in blender until thoroughly combined.

4. Transfer mixture to a heavy saucepan. Bring to a boil over medium-high heat. Reduce heat and simmer for 15 minutes.

5. Add soy cheese if desired and stir well.

Storing Pesto

Most pesto freezes very well. Instead of freezing the whole batch of pesto, freeze it in portion-sized amounts in individual containers with tight-fitting lids. Skip the cheese when freezing; add it right before serving.

Serves 8

2 medium tomatoes
1 sweet red pepper
2 tablespoons minced fresh parsley
2 cloves garlic
¼ cup chopped fresh basil leaves
1 tablespoon plus 1½ teaspoons all-purpose flour
¼ teaspoon salt
⅛ teaspoon pepper
2 teaspoons grated soy cheese (optional)

Basil Pesto

Serves 16

2 cups fresh basil leaves
1 cup shredded Parmesan
　cheese
3 cloves garlic, peeled
½ cup pine nuts
½ cup extra-virgin olive oil
Salt and pepper to taste

This pesto is best when it is used fresh. Don't plan to store it in the refrigerator for more than three days! This is a low-lactose recipe, but *not* a no-lactose recipe. Parmesan cheese has a low lactose count, but if you are exceptionally sensitive, it could bother you. Make sure you know your own tendencies and limits with dairy!

1. Wash basil leaves and blot dry using paper towels. Remove any long stems and discard.

2. Add the Parmesan, garlic, and pine nuts to a food processor or blender and process until the mixture is coarsely ground.

3. Add basil and process until entire mixture is coarsely ground. While blender is running, slowly add the oil in a thin stream.

4. When entire mixture is evenly blended to a coarse, chopped consistency, add salt and pepper to taste.

5. Store in the refrigerator or freeze in small amounts.

Black Bean Salsa

This black bean salsa is tasty rolled in a tortilla with some fresh greens and some grilled chicken.

1. Drain black beans and rinse under cold water. Coarsely chop the onion.

2. In a small bowl, mix black beans and onion.

3. Add remaining ingredients and thoroughly mix.

4. Let stand for at least 60 minutes before serving to allow the flavors to mingle.

5. Serve at room temperature or chilled. If refrigerating, be sure to cover tightly.

Serves 10

1 cup canned black beans
2 tablespoons white onion
2 cloves minced garlic
⅛ teaspoon dried oregano
¼ teaspoon ground cumin
2 teaspoons chopped fresh cilantro
¾ teaspoon freshly squeezed lime juice

Stove-Top Apple Butter

Yields 56 servings

12 large Granny Smith apples
1 cup frozen apple juice
    concentrate
2 tablespoons lemon juice
1 cup brown sugar
1½ teaspoons cinnamon
¼ teaspoon salt
¼ teaspoon allspice
Pinch ground cloves

So many decadent breakfast treats have lactose. This one doesn't, and it's one of the best things you'll ever taste! Apple butter is a great replacement for butter or margarine on toast.

1. Peel, core, and slice the apples. Place in a large, heavy kettle. Add apple juice concentrate to apples.

2. Place over medium heat and bring the mixture to a boil. Reduce the heat and simmer until apples are tender, about 20 minutes.

3. Place the hot mixture in a blender. Purée briefly; there should still be small chunks of apples in the mixture. Return the mixture to the kettle. Add lemon juice, brown sugar, cinnamon, salt, allspice, and ground cloves.

4. Cook over low heat until mixture thickens, about 30 minutes. Be sure to stir often so mixture doesn't stick; apple butter scorches easily!

5. Allow to cool to room temperature and store in glass jars.

Granny Smith

One of the world's most famous apple varieties, Granny Smiths are bright green and shiny. They are very juicy and have a slightly tangy flavor. Granny Smiths were first cultivated in Australia in 1865 by Marie Ana Smith. They slowly made their way around the world, reaching the United States more than one hundred years after they were first cultivated.

Yogurt Mint Sauce

Fresh mint in almost anything is so refreshing! This sauce can be a complement to an entrée or a great sauce or dip for fresh fruits or veggies.

1. Combine all ingredients in a medium-sized bowl.

2. Stir until well blended.

3. Cover tightly and chill thoroughly. Serve chilled.

Ah, Mint!

Can you smell it? Just reading the word conjures up the aroma and fresh smell of mint! Although the taste of mint is somewhat warm, its aftertaste is cool and refreshing. Its flavor is used in breath fresheners and candies, but fresh mint has its own strong, unique flavor.

Serves 8

1 cup plain soy yogurt
¼ cup chopped fresh mint
2 tablespoons freshly
    squeezed lemon juice

Dilled Mustard Sauce

Serves 8

1 (8-ounce) carton plain soy
 yogurt
2 tablespoons Dijon mustard
1 teaspoon chopped fresh
 chives
1 teaspoon Worcestershire
 sauce
1 teaspoon lemon juice
½ teaspoon dried whole dill
 weed
Fresh dill sprig (optional)

Want to wake up your freshly steamed veggies? This homemade dilled mustard sauce
will do it!

1. In a small bowl, combine yogurt, mustard,
chives, Worcestershire sauce, lemon juice, and
dill weed. Mix well.

2. Cover tightly and chill.

3. Transfer to a serving container, and garnish
with dill sprig, if desired.

4. Serve chilled mustard sauce over chicken,
fish, or vegetables.

Tomato Fresca Sauce

Try this incredibly fresh sauce over spaghetti squash.

1. In a medium-sized bowl, combine tomatoes, garlic, salt, oregano, and basil. Mix well.

2. Add oil, mixing thoroughly.

3. Serve at room temperature. Store any extra sauce in the refrigerator for one day.

Serves 8

2 cups diced fresh tomato
2 cloves minced garlic
1 teaspoon salt
¼ teaspoon dried oregano
1 tablespoon finely chopped
    fresh basil
¾ teaspoon canola oil

Mushroom Sauce

Serves 8

3 tablespoons margarine
¼ cup flour
1 cup warm soy milk
¾ pound fresh button mush-
    rooms, thinly sliced
1 tablespoon cream sherry
¼ teaspoon salt
⅛ teaspoon ground white
    pepper

As smooth as velvet with a slightly sweet flavor, this sauce can be spooned over steak, chicken, or freshly steamed veggies.

1. In a large saucepan, melt margarine over low heat. Whisking constantly, add flour and cook until it is smoothly combined and bub-bling (about 1 minute).

2. Gradually whisk in the soy milk, ½ cup at a time. Continue whisking constantly for about 5 minutes or until sauce begins to thicken. Don't allow sauce to boil.

3. Blend in mushrooms. Cover and continue simmering, stirring occasionally. Allow to cook for 7 minutes or until the mixture is reduced by half.

4. Remove saucepan from heat. Stir in sherry, salt, and pepper, blending until smooth. Serve hot.

Spicy Tofu Sauce

Depending on your level of tolerance for spiciness, you may want to start out with half a serrano chili.

1. Place garlic and chili in a blender and chop.

2. Add olive oil and blend flavors.

3. Rinse tofu and blot with paper towel. Break into pieces and add to spiced oil in blender.

4. Add vinegar, basil, salt, and fresh ginger. Blend all ingredients well.

5. If mixture is too thick, slowly add water until desired consistency is reached.

Hot, Hot, Hot!

Cooking with chilies can give your food incredible flavor, but you must be careful! Make sure to thoroughly wash your hands after seeding or cutting chilies; use rubber gloves if you're worried about your skin coming into contact with the oils from the chilies. Definitely avoid rubbing your eyes or nose before washing your hands—the oil can burn!

Serves 5

2 cloves garlic
1 small serrano chili
⅛ cup olive oil
½ cup firm tofu
⅛ cup white wine vinegar
1 tablespoon dried basil
½ teaspoon vegetable salt
1 teaspoon freshly grated ginger
⅛ cup water

Bordelaise Sauce

Serves 4

1 tablespoon margarine
1 tablespoon all-purpose flour
½ cup water
1 tablespoon plus 1½ tea-
spoons dry red wine
1½ teaspoons minced green
onion
1½ teaspoons minced fresh
parsley
1 bay leaf
½ teaspoon beef-flavored
bouillon granules
⅛ teaspoon dried whole
thyme
Freshly ground black pepper
to taste

A rich, tangy sauce that's a perfect complement to lamb, beef, or other red meat. It's so
savory, and completely lactose-free!

1. In a small saucepan, melt margarine over
low heat.

2. Gradually add flour, stirring constantly until
smooth (about 1 minute). Slowly add water
and wine. Stir constantly until sauce reaches a
smooth consistency.

3. Stir in onion, parsley, bay leaf, bouillon granules, thyme, and pepper. Cook over medium-
high heat, stirring constantly, until thickened
and bubbly.

4. Remove bay leaf.

5. Serve sauce warm over lamb chops or
other entrée.

Beans and Lentils

chapter eight

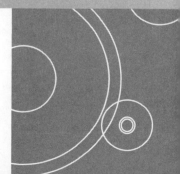

Five-Bean Salad

Serves 10

1 (16-ounce) can green beans
1 (16-ounce) can yellow wax beans
1 (15-ounce) can red kidney beans
1 (16-ounce) can garbanzo beans
1 (16-ounce) can pinto beans
½ cup chopped green pepper
½ cup chopped celery
½ cup finely chopped onion
⅓ cup sugar
⅔ cup tarragon vinegar
2 tablespoons olive oil
½ teaspoon salt
½ teaspoon garlic salt

Be sure to allow this salad to refrigerate for several hours and let the flavors mingle. This is one of those recipes that is always better the next day!

1. Combine all the beans, green pepper, celery, and onion in a large bowl.

2. Mix the sugar, vinegar, oil, salt, and garlic salt in a small bowl.

3. Pour the dressing mixture over the vegetables and stir gently.

4. Refrigerate for at least 6 hours. Stir several times while chilling so flavors mingle evenly.

Bean and Lentil Trivia

Beans and lentils have been found in 5,000-year-old settlements in the Eastern Mediterranean, in Egyptian pyramids, Hungarian caves, Britain, and Switzerland, and in even earlier civilizations such as those in Peru, the Middle East, and eastern India. Beans and lentils are thought to have originated from the wild lentils that still grow in India, Turkey, and other Middle Eastern countries.

Rice and Bean Salad

A variety of beans coupled with rice, this salad is easy to prepare and chock full of great nutrients. It's another overnighter; keep this salad in the fridge to allow the flavors to penetrate. It's worth the wait!

1. Drain both cans of beans.

2. Combine beans, rice, peas, celery, onion, and green chilies in a large bowl.

3. Pour salad dressing over the ingredients in the bowl. Toss, coating evenly.

4. Cover and refrigerate for 24 hours before serving.

Serves 12

1 (16-ounce) can pinto beans
1 (15-ounce) can black beans
3 cups cooked rice of choice
1 (10-ounce) package frozen green peas, thawed
1 cup sliced celery
1 cup chopped onion
2 (4-ounce) cans chopped green chilies
1 (8-ounce) bottle Italian salad dressing

Tex-Mex Black Bean Dip

Serves 6

2 (15-ounce) cans black
    beans, drained
1 teaspoon olive oil
1 cup onion, chopped
4 cloves garlic, minced
1 cup fresh tomato, chopped
⅔ cup salsa
1 teaspoon ground cumin
1 teaspoon chili powder
½ cup shredded soy cheese
    (optional)
½ cup cilantro, chopped
2 tablespoons fresh lime juice

Serve this tangy dip with tortilla chips.

1. Place black beans in a bowl. Partially mash beans until chunky. Set aside.

2. Heat oil over medium-high heat in a non-stick skillet. Add onion and garlic. Sauté until tender, about 4 minutes.

3. Add beans, tomatoes, salsa, ground cumin, and chili powder. Stirring constantly, cook until mixture thickens, about 5 minutes.

4. Remove from heat. Add soy cheese if desired.

5. Stir in fresh cilantro and lime juice. Serve warm or at room temperature.

Layered Four-Bean Salad

This is a crowd-pleasing picnic dish! If you prepare it for a picnic, skip the glass dish and use a large plastic bowl with a top that seals.

1. Cook all dry beans according to package directions. Drain and chill beans.

2. Mix sugar, vinegar, oil, parsley, mustard, basil, oregano, salt, and pepper in a small bowl. Set aside.

3. Line a large glass bowl with romaine lettuce leaves.

4. Place a layer of black beans on bottom of bowl. Drizzle with ¼ of the dressing.

5. Add the navy beans and drizzle with more dressing. Continue until you have four layers.

6. Garnish top with red onion rings. Chill thoroughly.

Bean Cooking Hints

Cooking beans is kind of like a treasure hunt. Before you cook them, be sure to pick through the beans and remove any stones, broken beans, or other foreign objects. It isn't surprising to find a bit of the bean field in the bag with your dried beans.

Serves 24

1 pound black beans
1 pound navy beans
1 pound pinto beans
1 pound lima beans
½ cup sugar
½ cup red wine vinegar
½ cup light olive oil
2 tablespoons fresh parsley, chopped
½ teaspoon dry mustard
2 teaspoons fresh basil
½ teaspoon oregano
Salt and freshly ground black pepper to taste
Romaine lettuce leaves
1 medium red onion, sliced and separated into rings

Old-Fashioned Pot O' Beans Made New

Serves 8

1 pound great northern dried
   beans
2 quarts water
1 medium onion, minced
2 cloves garlic, minced
2 carrots, sliced
½ cup chopped celery
 3 (4-ounce) smoked pork
   chops
½ teaspoon black pepper
2 teaspoons salt
1 teaspoon brown sugar
1 tablespoon prepared
   mustard

Old-fashioned beans usually called for fat ham hocks for flavor and lots of greasy goop. This updated recipe calls for smoked pork chops in place of the ham hocks, and if you want to skip the pork chops, please do!

1. Wash and drain the beans. Place in a large kettle with 2 quarts water. Let soak overnight.

2. Drain beans and cover with fresh water.

3. Add onion, garlic, carrots, and celery. Cover and simmer slowly for 2 hours. Stir occasionally. Add more water as needed, checking the level often.

4. Trim and cube pork chops. Add pepper, smoked pork chops, salt, brown sugar, and mustard. Simmer for another 45–60 minutes until flavors blend.

Cherry Tomatoes with Bean Stuffing

Stuffing cherry tomatoes with this flavorful and tasty bean stuffing is well worth the time it takes. They are great at a party or a barbecue!

1. Rinse tomatoes and set aside. Wash all basil. Set aside 24 small basil leaves. Chop remaining basil.

2. Cut 12 tomatoes in half. Squeeze out all the seeds and juice. Dice tomatoes and set aside.

3. In a blender, purée beans, basil leaves, garlic oil, and lemon juice until finely chopped. Transfer bean mixture to a medium bowl. Stir in chopped tomatoes and chopped basil, mixing well.

4. Cut off top quarter of remaining 24 tomatoes. Gently squeeze out the seeds, liquid, and pulp using a small spoon to create a cavity in the tomato.

5. Fill tomatoes with the bean mixture, again using a small spoon. Garnish each tomato with a fresh basil leaf.

Yields 24

36 cherry tomatoes, divided
1 bunch fresh basil plus 24 leaves
1 (15-ounce) can cannellini beans, drained
2 tablespoons garlic-flavored olive oil
2 tablespoons freshly squeezed lemon juice

Cannellini Beans

Cannellini beans are very popular in Italy, especially in Tuscany, where the people living there have been affectionately nicknamed mangiafagiole—"beaneaters"! Cannellini beans are sometimes referred to as white kidney beans and are related to navy and great northern beans. They have a very mellow flavor. Feel free to use them interchangeably with other white beans.

Many-Bean Soup

Serves 8

¼ pound dried white kidney
  beans, soaked and rinsed
½ pound dried fava beans,
  soaked and rinsed
¼ pound dried garbanzos
  (chickpeas)
¼ pound dried lentils, any
  color
¼ pound dried split yellow
  peas
9–10 cups water
1 (5-ounce) can water chestnuts, drained and sliced
3 ribs celery, chopped
1 medium onion, diced
1 medium carrot, chopped
6 dry sundried tomatoes,
  finely chopped
2 garlic cloves, mashed
3 teaspoons ground fennel
  seeds
Salt and pepper to taste
Seasoned croutons (optional)

This is an awesome winter soup to simmer on the stove for hours. It fills the house with warm, cozy aromas and will warm tummies when it's done!

1. Soak, rinse, and drain legumes. Place in a large soup pot and cover with water.

2. Bring to a boil over medium-high heat. Reduce heat and simmer for about 1½ hours.

3. Add water chestnuts, celery, onion, carrot, tomatoes, garlic, and fennel.

4. Continue simmering for another 1½–2 hours over low heat until all legumes are tender.

5. Ladle soup into soup bowls, season to taste with salt and pepper. Top with seasoned croutons if desired. Serve immediately.

Turkey Black Bean Chili

Black beans are a great staple in any pantry. Not only do they have a great flavor, but it's hard to imagine anything that tastes this good is also good for you!

1. Coat a small Dutch oven with cooking spray. Add olive oil. Heat over medium-high heat.

2. Add onion and celery. Sauté until tender. Allow to cool slightly.

3. Place mixture in a blender. Drain beans, reserving liquid. Add half the beans with all the liquid to blender. Process until smooth. Stop once and scrape down sides.

4. Return mixture to Dutch oven. Add remaining beans, tomato, chilies, turkey, and chili seasoning. Cook over medium heat until heated thoroughly.

5. Ladle into bowls. Top evenly with yogurt. Garnish with pepper strips, if desired.

Serves 6

Nonstick cooking spray
1 tablespoon olive oil
1 cup coarsely chopped onion
½ cup sliced celery
2 (15-ounce) cans black beans
1 (10-ounce) can diced tomatoes and green chilies, undrained
6 ounces cooked turkey breast, diced
1 tablespoon chili seasoning mix
¼ cup plus 1 tablespoon plain soy yogurt
Sweet red pepper strips (optional)

Garbanzos and Rice

Serves 4

1½ cups canned garbanzo
   beans
2 cups cooked rice
1 teaspoon salt
1 teaspoon margarine
⅓ cup honey
⅓ cup brown sugar
¼ teaspoon cinnamon

Choose your favorite rice for this recipe.
Serve it warm as a dessert with honey, brown
sugar, and cinnamon.

1. Preheat oven to 350°F.

2. Combine all ingredients except cinnamon in
a medium-sized bowl, blending thoroughly.

3. Pour mixture into a casserole dish. Dust
with cinnamon.

4. Bake for 25 minutes.

Mediterranean Eggplant and Garbanzos

If you have an electric skillet, heat it to 300°F and cook all ingredients together for about 30 minutes instead of using the heavy skillet.

1. Wash whole eggplant and prick skin in several places with a fork. Place on paper towel in microwave oven. Precook in microwave on high for 8 minutes.

2. Set eggplant aside to cool. When cool to touch, cut in thick slices. Cover with damp paper towel. Seed and slice red bell pepper.

3. Put olive oil in a heavy skillet over medium-high heat. When oil is hot, add onions, garlic, and bell pepper. Sauté until soft.

4. Add eggplant slices, zucchini, beans, tomatoes, canned tomatoes, and spices. Cook until eggplant and zucchini are tender, about 45 minutes.

Garbanzo Bean Trivia

Garbanzo beans are also referred to as chickpeas. Like most beans, garbanzo beans are rich in soluble fiber, the best sort of fiber. Soluble fiber helps eliminate cholesterol from the body. Garbanzos are a good source of folate, vitamin E, potassium, iron, manganese, copper, zinc, and calcium. As a high-potassium, low-sodium food, they can help reduce blood pressure.

Serves 6

1 large eggplant
1 large red bell pepper
2 tablespoons olive oil
2 medium onions, sliced
2 garlic cloves, mashed
2 medium zucchini, sliced
2 cups cooked garbanzos, drained
2 medium tomatoes, cut into eighths
1 (16-ounce) can tomatoes, drained and chopped
½ teaspoon dried turmeric
½ teaspoon oregano
½ teaspoon thyme
1 teaspoon ground cinnamon

New Potatoes and Beans

Serves 6

2 cups water
3 cups sliced new red
   potatoes
¼ cup chopped onion
2 teaspoons instant chicken
   bouillon granules
1 clove garlic, minced
1 (15-ounce) can red kidney
   beans
¼ cup green pepper strips
¼ cup red pepper strips
1 tablespoon olive oil
1 tablespoon red wine vinegar
2 teaspoons dried parsley
   flakes
¼ teaspoon dried rosemary
   leaves, crushed

The flavor of new, small red potatoes just can't be beat. This is a good barbecue dish that makes a very colorful presentation and brings folks back for a second helping!

1. Bring water to a boil in a 3-quart saucepan over high heat.

2. Add potatoes, onion, bouillon, and garlic to boiling water. Return to boil.

3. Reduce heat to low and cover. Cook for about 10 minutes until potatoes are crisp-tender. Drain.

4. Rinse and drain red kidney beans. Cut green and red pepper into ¼" strips. Add kidney beans, pepper strips, olive oil, vinegar, parsley flakes, and rosemary leaves to potato mixture. Stir well to combine all ingredients. Return to medium heat.

5. Cook, uncovered, for about 3 minutes or until hot. Stir occasionally to prevent sticking. Remove from heat and cover. Let stand for 5 minutes before serving.

Tortillas and Black Beans

This is a very satisfying and filling dish with high calcium scores, low lactose scores, and great flavor and taste!

1. Cook rice according to package directions. While rice is cooking, prepare the rest of the recipe. Rinse black beans and set aside.

2. Heat olive oil in a large skillet or wok. Add onion and sauté for 1 minute.

3. Add garlic and sauté for another 2 minutes. Add bell pepper to skillet and continue sautéing for another 2 minutes. Add jalapeño pepper, chopped tomato, cumin, beans, and cooked rice. Keep mixture warm.

4. Heat tortillas in oven or microwave according to package directions. Fill your warm tortilla with mixture.

5. Garnish with condiments of your choice

Serves 8

1 cup basmati rice
2 (15-ounce) cans black beans
1 tablespoon olive oil
1 medium yellow onion, chopped
1 large clove garlic, minced
1 bell pepper, chopped
1 jalapeño pepper, chopped
1 Roma tomato, chopped
1 teaspoon cumin
1 package 8" flour tortillas
Chopped avocado, fresh cilantro, hot sauce, soy yogurt (optional)

No-Guilt Refried Beans

Serves 4

1 (15-ounce) can pinto beans
¼ cup thick and chunky salsa
2 tablespoons finely chopped
  onion
⅛ teaspoon garlic powder
1 tablespoon margarine

Just a little note on pinto beans: You can find them in the freezer section and make an awesome bean soup with them. Bean soups all taste thick and creamy, but without any of the actual dairy that would upset a lactose-sensitive stomach.

1. Drain and rinse pinto beans.

2. Combine beans, salsa, onion, and garlic powder in a heavy 2-quart saucepan over medium-high heat. Bring mixture to a boil, stirring occasionally.

3. Reduce heat to medium-low and simmer until onion is translucent, about 8 minutes. Stir occasionally to prevent sticking. Add margarine and stir until melted.

4. Remove from heat and allow mixture to cool slightly.

5. Pour mixture into a blender. Process until smooth.

Triple Bean Bake

If you like a little sweetness in your beans, then go for the addition of the light molasses. If you opt out of the molasses, the dry mustard combined with the apple juice concentrate will give the flavor a new twist!

1. Preheat oven to 375°F. Drain and rinse all beans.

2. Put oil in a 10-inch nonstick skillet over medium heat. Add onion and celery. Cook until tender, about 6 minutes, stirring occasionally.

3. Add pinto beans, butter beans, garbanzo beans, tomato sauce, apple juice, dry mustard, and molasses, if desired. Stir until combined.

4. Spoon mixture into a 2-quart casserole dish. Bake covered until hot and bubbly, about 30 minutes.

Serves 8

1 (15-ounce) can pinto beans
1 (15-ounce) can butter beans
1 (15-ounce) can garbanzo
  beans
1 teaspoon light olive oil
1 cup thinly sliced onion
½ cup thinly sliced celery
1 (8-ounce) can tomato sauce
¼ cup frozen apple juice
  concentrate, defrosted
½ teaspoon dry mustard
1 tablespoon light molasses
  (optional)

Lentil Stew

Serves 8

2 large onions, chopped
2 medium carrots, chopped
1 cup dry lentils
½ cup chopped fresh parsley
1 (16-ounce) can whole
   tomatoes, undrained and
   coarsely chopped
3 cups chicken broth
¼ cup dry sherry
½ teaspoon dried whole thyme
½ teaspoon dried whole
   marjoram
½ teaspoon pepper

This stew will warm your very soul on a cold winter day!

1. Combine all ingredients in a large soup pot. Bring to a boil.

2. Reduce heat and cover.

3. Simmer over low heat until lentils are tender, about 45 minutes.

4. Serve piping hot!

Legacy of Lentils

Lentils, also referred to as "dal," are the staple food in every home in India. Dal is India's comfort food! A variety of lentils exist with colors that range from yellow to red-orange to green, brown, and black.

Lentil Salad

The colors of the lentils in this salad make it very inviting. The combination of lentils with spinach torn in small pieces gets very high ratings on the healthy scale!

1. Cook the lentils according to package directions. Drain and chill the lentils.

2. In a small bowl, combine onion, salsa, chili powder, oregano, and lemon juice. Set aside.

3. Put torn spinach and salsa mixture in a medium bowl. Toss until mixed well.

4. Fold in lentils.

5. Place whole spinach leaves on 4 salad plates. Mound salad on top.

Serves 4

½ cup red lentils, cooked, drained, and chilled
½ cup yellow lentils, cooked, drained and chilled
½ cup mild onion, finely chopped
½ cup mild salsa
2 teaspoons chili powder
½ teaspoon dried oregano
2 tablespoons lemon juice
1 cup fresh spinach, torn
Whole spinach leaves (optional)

Lentils and Rice

Serves 6

1 tablespoon margarine
2 tablespoons olive oil
2 cups sliced onions
1 cup lentils, rinsed
5 cups water
3 cups chicken or vegetable
    broth
½ cup long-grain rice
¾ teaspoon salt
1 teaspoon ground cumin
Freshly ground black pepper
    to taste

If you're accustomed to using veggie broth in your cooking, use it in this recipe as well. Veggie broth enhances the flavor of this hearty, filling no-lactose dish.

1. Heat margarine and oil together until margarine melts in a large, heavy skillet over low heat. Add onion slices. Cook slowly, stirring.

2. Place water and lentils in a large stockpot and bring to a boil over medium-high heat. Reduce heat and simmer, covered, for 20 minutes.

3. Drain lentils and place in a large, heavy saucepan. Add broth, rice, salt, cumin, and pepper.

4. Set aside ⅓ cup of the onions. Add the remainder of the onions to the lentil mixture. Bring to a boil. Reduce heat and cook, covered, until rice is tender, about 25 minutes.

5. Sprinkle the reserved onions over the top and serve immediately.

Appetizers

chapter nine

Crisp Polenta Squares

Serves 4–6

3 cups water
1 cup tomato juice
4 cloves garlic, minced
1 teaspoon salt
⅛ teaspoon pepper
1 cup cornmeal
½ cup olive oil

Polenta is made from cornmeal that has been cooked until soft. When chilled, sliced, and fried, it becomes a crisp and delectable snack.

1. In a large saucepan, combine water, tomato juice, garlic, salt, and pepper and bring to a boil. Stir in cornmeal; cook and stir over low heat until very thick, about 12–17 minutes.

2. Pour mixture into oiled baking dish; spread about ½" thick. Cover and chill until very firm.

3. When ready to eat, cut into 2" squares. Heat olive oil over medium-high heat until about 375°F. Fry polenta squares, a few at a time, until very crisp. Drain on paper towels. Serve with any spicy salsa or dip.

Crispy Rice Balls

Fry these little balls as your guests arrive. They're crisp and savory, with a tender center. Try molding the rice around a tiny square of soy or lactose-free cheese before frying.

1. In a medium saucepan, combine rice and water. Bring to a boil over high heat, then reduce heat to low; simmer for 18–23 minutes, or until rice is tender and water is absorbed.

2. Meanwhile, heat olive oil over medium heat. Add onion; cook and stir until onion begins to brown, about 8–9 minutes. Stir in garlic for 1 minute, then stir into hot cooked rice. Let cool for 30 minutes, then add egg, salt, pepper, horseradish, and thyme.

3. Form mixture into 1" balls; roll in crushed cereal to coat.

4. Heat oil in a heavy skillet over medium heat. Fry rice balls, turning carefully, until golden brown and crisp, about 4–5 minutes. Drain on paper towels to serve.

Serves 8

1 cup medium-grain rice
2 cups water
1 tablespoon olive oil
½ cup minced onion
3 cloves garlic, minced
1 egg
½ teaspoon salt
⅛ teaspoon cayenne pepper
2 tablespoons prepared horseradish
½ teaspoon dried thyme leaves
1 cup crushed puffed-rice cereal
1 cup vegetable oil

Cooking Rice

There are three main types of rice: long grain, medium grain, and short grain. They differ in the amount and kind of starch they contain. Long-grain rice cooks up fluffier because it has less amylopectin, which is the starch that makes rice sticky. Medium-grain rice has more amylopectin, so it is stickier, suitable for rice balls and risotto.

Dairy-Free Olive Cheese Ball

Serves 6–8

1 tablespoon olive oil
½ cup finely chopped onion
2 cloves garlic, minced
2 tablespoons Dijon mustard
¼ cup finely chopped black
    olives
1½ cups soy cream cheese
¼ cup finely chopped flat-leaf
    parsley

If your lactose intolerance is a mild case, you might find that you can make this with softened cream cheese instead. Choose your favorite olives, and serve with crisp crackers.

1. In a small saucepan, heat olive oil over medium heat. Add onion and garlic; cook and stir until onion starts to brown, about 8–10 minutes. Remove from heat, place onions and garlic in a small bowl, and let cool for 20 minutes.

2. Add mustard and black olives and stir to combine. Add soy cream cheese. Cover and chill until firm, about 1–2 hours. Then form into a ball and roll in parsley to coat.

Lactose-Free Cheese Balls

Serve these delicious little spicy balls as part of an antipasto tray.

1. Place the "cream cheese" in a small bowl; mix in paprika and pepper. Roll mixture into 1" balls; roll in herbs; place on a serving plate.

2. Drizzle with olive oil and refrigerate for 1–2 hours to blend flavors before serving.

Antipasto

The word literally means "before the meal." Antipasto usually consists of smoked and brined meats, a variety of cheeses, and pickled, marinated, and raw vegetables. You can also include breads on an antipasto platter, especially rustic Italian and French breads.

Serves 4–6

1 cup soy-based or lactose-free cream cheese
½ teaspoon paprika
⅛ teaspoon pepper
2 tablespoons minced cilantro
2 tablespoons fresh minced basil
3 tablespoons extra-virgin olive oil

Grilled Shrimp Skewers

Serves 4–6

2 tablespoons olive oil
2 onions
2 tablespoons lemon juice
2 tablespoons Dijon mustard
½ teaspoon dried thyme
   leaves
1½ pounds large raw shrimp
½ teaspoon salt
⅛ teaspoon pepper

Mustard and lemon juice flavor tender shrimp in this easy recipe. You could use cubes of chicken or turkey instead of the shrimp for a fish-free recipe, if you have picky eaters at home.

1. Place olive oil in a medium pan over medium heat. Cut onions into quarters, then cut each quarter in half to make 16 wedges. Cook in oil, turning carefully to keep the wedges together, for 4–5 minutes to soften.

2. Remove pan from heat, then remove onions from pan and set aside. Add lemon juice, mustard, and thyme to olive oil and mix well. Add shrimp and stir to coat.

3. String shrimp and onion wedges on skewers; brush with any remaining mustard mixture and sprinkle with salt and pepper.

4. Preheat broiler until hot. Cook 6 inches from broiler, turning once, until shrimp curl and turn pink and onions are slightly charred, about 4–5 minutes. Serve immediately.

Corn Quesadillas

Corn tortillas are a great choice for appetizers, to make your own chips, and to use as the bread for sandwich wraps.

1. In a small saucepan, heat olive oil over medium heat. Add garlic and jalapeños; cook and stir for 2–3 minutes, until softened. Add corn; cook and stir for 4–5 minutes longer, until hot. Remove from heat and stir in black beans and salsa.

2. Arrange half of the tortillas on work surface. Spread each with some of the lactose-free cheese. Divide corn mixture among tortillas, then top with the remaining tortillas.

3. Heat a large skillet or griddle over medium heat. Grill quesadillas, turning once, until cheese melts and tortillas are toasted. Cut into wedges and serve with more salsa.

Soy Cheese

Soy cheeses don't melt as well as dairy cheese. They can also be rather bland. You can solve these problems by looking for flavored soy cheeses. Also, when adding the cheese to a recipe that is heated, add the cheese at the very end and cover the food while it cooks. The steam produced will help soften the cheese.

Serves 6

1 tablespoon olive oil
3 cloves garlic, minced
2 jalapeño peppers, minced
1½ cups frozen corn
1 (15-ounce) can black beans, drained and rinsed
½ cup jarred salsa
12 (6-inch) corn tortillas
½ cup lactose-free or soy cheese, shredded
1 cup shredded dairy-free pepper jack soy cheese

Roasted Sweet and Spicy "Nuts"

Yields 3 cups; Serves 6

2 cups dried soybeans
6 cups water
⅓ cup honey
1 tablespoon curry powder
1 teaspoon fine salt

This is an interesting way to make an alternative to the roasted, flavored nuts you can buy in the supermarket. Not only is it lactose-free, of course, but it's actually healthier than the peanuts you might otherwise be eating.

1. Pick over soybeans, discarding any that are shriveled, and any extraneous material. Rinse them in cold water, drain, then place in a large bowl. Cover with water and let soak for 12 hours.

2. Preheat oven to 325°F. Drain soybeans and pat dry with paper towels. Place in a single layer on a large cookie sheet. Roast for 55–65 minutes, turning with a spatula every 10 minutes, until crisp and light golden brown. Remove from cookie sheet; let stand on paper towels for 10 minutes.

3. Return soybeans to cookie sheet and drizzle with honey. Toss to coat, then sprinkle with curry powder and salt.

4. Reduce oven temperature to 275°F. Roast the seasoned soybeans for another 30–40 minutes, stirring every 8 minutes, until crisp. Let cool, then store in an airtight container.

Sausage Bruschetta

This is another appetizer that will fool people into thinking you've used real cheese.

1. Preheat broiler. In a medium saucepan, cook sausage, onion, and bell pepper over medium heat, stirring to break up sausage, until meat is cooked. Drain thoroughly.

2. Spread 1 ounce cream cheese on each slice of French bread. Top with sausage mixture and sprinkle with soy cheese. Place bruschetta on broiler pan. Broil 6 inches from heat source until cheese bubbles and begins to brown. Serve immediately.

Serves 12

½ pound ground spicy pork sausage
1 onion, chopped
½ cup chopped red bell pepper
1 (8-ounce) lactose-free cream cheese, softened
12 slices French Bread (Chapter 4)
1 cup shredded soy cheese

Chicken Mushroom Tartlets

Yields 32 tartlets

1 boneless, skinless chicken breast, diced
2 tablespoons flour
½ teaspoon salt
⅛ teaspoon pepper
1 tablespoon olive oil
1 onion, chopped
1 cup sliced button mushrooms
1 tablespoon lemon juice
½ teaspoon dried thyme leaves
¼ cup mayonnaise
½ cup chopped cherry tomatoes
32 frozen mini tartlet shells

These elegant little appetizers are the perfect first course for a dinner party or trendy meal. They're small yet satisfying, and of course, they have no lactose! Make sure you buy the mushrooms as close to when you're planning to cook this dish as possible, or else they can quickly begin to soften.

1. Preheat oven to 375°F. Toss chicken with flour, salt, and pepper. Heat olive oil in a medium skillet and add chicken; cook and stir until thoroughly cooked, about 4–6 minutes. Remove chicken from skillet with slotted spoon and set aside in a medium bowl.

2. Add onion to skillet; cook and stir until it begins to brown around the edges, about 8–10 minutes. Add mushrooms; cook and stir until tender, about 4–5 minutes longer. Remove half of this mixture to a food processor; process until smooth and thick.

3. Add to chicken in bowl along with unprocessed onion and mushrooms, lemon juice, thyme, mayonnaise, and tomatoes; stir well to mix. Fill each tartlet shell with about 2 teaspoons filling; place on a cookie sheet.

4. Bake for 9–14 minutes, or until filling is hot and shells are golden brown. Cool for 10 minutes, then serve.

Tartlet Shells

You can sometimes find tartlet shells in the bakery or frozen foods aisle of the supermarket, but if you have a pie-crust recipe you like, use that to make the little shells. You can roll out the dough and cut 2" rounds, fit those in the miniature muffin cups, and bake, or roll the dough into ¾" balls and press into the muffin cups.

Stuffed Cherry Tomatoes

You can flavor the basic filling any way you'd like: Add jalapeño peppers, chopped toasted nuts, tiny shrimp, cooked ground ham, or pepperoni.

1. Cut the tops off each cherry tomato; using a small serrated spoon or melon scoop, remove pulp and discard. Put tomatoes upside-down on paper towel–lined plates to drain.

2. In a small bowl, combine remaining ingredients except parsley, and mix well to blend. Spoon or pipe filling into each cherry tomato.

3. To serve, place parsley on a serving plate and arrange tomatoes on top. Cover with plastic wrap and chill for at least 1 hour before serving.

Yields 24 appetizers

2 pints cherry tomatoes
1 cup soy cheese
⅓ cup mayonnaise
1 tablespoon prepared horse-
   radish
1 tablespoon lemon juice
¼ cup finely chopped ripe
   olives, if desired
⅓ cup chopped flat-leaf
   parsley

Stuffed Bacon Mushrooms

Serves 8

16 large button mushrooms
Olive oil, as needed
4 slices bacon
1 onion, chopped
4 cloves garlic, minced
½ cup seasoned bread crumbs
⅔ cup lactose-free cream cheese
⅛ teaspoon cayenne pepper
¼ cup chopped flat-leaf parsley

These bacon mushrooms will be the star of the show at any cocktail party, regardless of whether or not they go up against non-lactose-free recipes!

1. Remove stems from mushrooms; trim ends of the stems and coarsely chop. Place mushrooms gill side up on a baking sheet and brush with olive oil. Preheat oven to 350°F.

2. Cook bacon in a medium skillet over medium heat until crisp. Remove bacon to paper towels to drain and crumble; set aside. Remove all but 1 tablespoon bacon drippings from skillet.

3. Cook mushroom stems, onion, and garlic in bacon drippings until tender, about 6–7 minutes. Remove from heat and stir in reserved bacon, bread crumbs, cream cheese, and cayenne pepper; mix well.

4. Stuff the mushroom caps with mixture. Bake for 15–20 minutes, or until the stuffing is hot and bubbly. Sprinkle with parsley and serve immediately.

Roasted Garlic

Roasted garlic cloves are a great spread on bread. They can be added to soy cream cheese for a sandwich spread or to any salsa recipe.

1. Preheat oven to 400°F. Cut garlic heads in half and place on aluminum foil, cut side up. Drizzle with olive oil and lemon juice and sprinkle with salt and pepper.

2. Wrap foil around garlic and place on a cookie sheet. Bake for 35–45 minutes, or until cloves are light brown and feel soft. Cool completely, then squeeze cloves out of their papery covering and refrigerate.

Roasted Garlic

Roasted garlic is a wonderful addition to a diet restricted by allergies. Studies have shown varied results, but the fact remains garlic is a good source of B vitamins, selenium, and manganese, and helps reduce cholesterol. When roasted, it becomes sweet and nutty. Freeze roasted garlic for up to 3 months.

Serves 6

2 heads garlic
2 tablespoons olive oil
2 teaspoons lemon juice
½ teaspoon salt
⅛ teaspoon pepper

Mashed Potatoes

Chopped Veggie Couscous

Sautéed Peas

Citrus Carrots

Apricot Glazed Beans

Rice Pilaf

Sautéed Yellow Squash and Carrots

Pesto Potatoes

Pea Sauté

Fried Rice

Hash Brown Casserole

Smashed Potatoes

Sparkly Carrots

Baked Squash

Veggie Risotto

Mashed Sweet Potatoes

Baked Rice Pilaf

Zucchini Stir-Fry

Sides

chapter ten

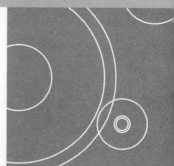

Mashed Potatoes

6 russet potatoes, peeled
2 tablespoons olive oil
1 onion, chopped
½–1 cup chicken stock
½ teaspoon salt
⅛ teaspoon white pepper

Mashed potatoes are true comfort food, and with this recipe anyone can eat them, even those who would normally be wary of the milk or cream that is often used. Full-flavored, full-bodied chicken stock here takes the place of the dairy. If you can make your own stock, that will take your potatoes to the next level!

1. Cut potatoes into chunks and place in a large pot. Cover with water and bring to a boil over high heat. Reduce heat to low, cover pot, and simmer for 9–15 minutes, or until potatoes are tender when tested with knife.

2. Meanwhile, in a small saucepan, heat olive oil over medium heat. Add onion; cook and stir until onions start to brown and caramelize, about 10–12 minutes.

3. When potatoes are cooked, drain and return to the hot pot. Set over medium heat and shake for a few minutes to dry potatoes. Add onion mixture and mash with a potato masher.

4. Gradually beat in enough stock until the potatoes are light and fluffy. Add salt and pepper to taste. Serve immediately.

Chopped Veggie Couscous

Use your favorite combination of vegetables in this easy side dish.

1. In a large skillet, heat olive oil over medium heat. Add onion and garlic; cook and stir for 4 minutes. Add bell pepper and mushrooms; cook and stir for 4–5 minutes longer, until crisp-tender.

2. Meanwhile, bring broth to a boil in a large saucepan. Add couscous, cover pan, remove from heat, and let stand for 5 minutes.

3. Add peas, salt, pepper, and thyme to vegetables in skillet; cook and stir for 4–5 minutes longer, until vegetables are tender.

4. Fluff couscous with a fork and add to skillet along with vinegar; stir gently to blend. Serve immediately.

Serves 8

2 tablespoons olive oil
1 onion, chopped
4 cloves garlic, minced
1 yellow bell pepper, chopped
1 cup chopped mushrooms
3 cups vegetable broth
2 cups couscous
1 cup frozen baby peas
½ teaspoon salt
⅛ teaspoon pepper
1 teaspoon dried thyme leaves
1 tablespoon balsamic vinegar

Sautéed Peas

Serves 6

1 tablespoon olive oil
2 shallots, minced
3 cloves garlic, minced
1 (16-ounce) bag frozen peas
2 tablespoons vegetable broth
½ teaspoon salt
⅛ teaspoon pepper
½ teaspoon dried thyme
  leaves

Baby peas are tender and sweet. Frozen peas can actually have more nutrients than fresh because they're processed right in the field.

1. In a large skillet, heat olive oil over medium heat. Add shallots and garlic; cook and stir until crisp-tender, about 4 minutes. Add peas and remaining ingredients and bring to a simmer.

2. Cover skillet and cook, stirring occasionally, until peas are hot and tender, about 8–11 minutes. Serve immediately.

Citrus Carrots

Citrus, in the form of juices and zest, brighten up carrots and mushrooms to turn this side dish into one worthy of company.

1. Place carrots in a skillet; cover with cold water. Bring to a boil, cover, reduce heat to low, and simmer for 3–4 minutes, until crisp-tender. Drain carrots and reserve; return skillet to heat.

2. Add olive oil to skillet along with garlic and mushrooms. Cook and stir for 4–5 minutes, until crisp-tender. Return carrots to skillet along with remaining ingredients.

3. Bring to a simmer; simmer for 2–3 minutes, or until vegetables are tender. Serve immediately.

Serves 6

1 (16-ounce) package baby carrots
2 tablespoons olive oil
3 cloves garlic, minced
1 cup chopped mushrooms
½ teaspoon salt
⅛ teaspoon white pepper
1 tablespoon lemon juice
2 tablespoons orange juice
1 teaspoon grated orange zest

Apricot Glazed Beans

Serves 4

1 pound green beans
1 tablespoon olive oil
1 shallot, minced
¼ cup apricot nectar
⅓ cup apricot preserves
2 teaspoons fresh chopped
    rosemary leaves
¼ teaspoon salt
Pinch white pepper

Green beans are often served plain; this recipe is a nice change of pace. It's a good side dish to serve with simple broiled chicken or pork chops.

1. Cook beans in a steamer until crisp-tender, about 4–5 minutes. Drain and set aside.

2. In a large saucepan, heat olive oil over medium heat. Add shallot; cook and stir until crisp-tender, about 4 minutes.

3. Add apricot nectar and beans; bring to a simmer. Cover pan and simmer for 3–4 minutes, until beans are tender. Uncover and add preserves, rosemary, salt, and pepper. Cook and stir for 1–2 minutes, until beans are glazed.

Rice Pilaf

Rice pilaf is an elegant side to a formal meal, and is a great go-to dish for a lactose-free home.

Serves 8

2 tablespoons olive oil
1 onion, chopped
3 cloves garlic, minced
½ cup chopped celery
2 cups uncooked long-grain rice
1 teaspoon salt
⅛ teaspoon pepper
4 cups vegetable broth

1. In a heavy saucepan, combine olive oil, onion, garlic, and celery. Cook and stir over medium heat until crisp-tender, about 5 minutes.

2. Add rice; cook and stir for 2 minutes longer. Sprinkle with salt and pepper.

3. Add vegetable broth. Bring to a boil, then reduce heat to low, cover saucepan, and cook for 15–20 minutes, or until rice is tender and broth is absorbed. Cover and remove from heat; let stand for 5 minutes. Fluff pilaf with a fork and serve.

Sautéed Yellow Squash and Carrots

Serves 6

2 tablespoons olive oil
2 shallots, minced
2 carrots, sliced
¼ cup water
3 yellow summer squash, sliced
½ teaspoon salt
⅛ teaspoon white pepper
½ teaspoon dried sage leaves

When the food on your plate is colorful, you know you're eating well. This side dish is a good example of a colorful recipe.

1. In a large saucepan, heat olive oil over medium heat. Add shallots; cook and stir for 2 minutes. Add carrots; cook and stir for 2 minutes. Add water and bring to a simmer. Cover saucepan; simmer for 3 minutes.

2. Add squash, stir, and raise heat. Simmer until liquid evaporates, stirring occasionally. Add salt, pepper, and sage leaves; cover and let stand off heat for 3 minutes. Stir and serve.

Summer Squash

There are two basic kinds of squash: summer and winter. Summer squash are thin-skinned and tender, cook quickly, and can be served raw. They include yellow squash and zucchini. Winter squash are hard, with thick shells, and they must be cooked before eating, like pumpkins, butternut squash, and acorn squash.

Pesto Potatoes

This flavorful side dish is delicious served with a steak or some grilled chicken or fish.

1. Preheat oven to 400°F. Scrub potatoes and cut into 1" pieces. Combine in a large roasting pan with olive oil, onion, and garlic. Roast for 30 minutes, then turn with a spatula. Roast for 30–40 minutes longer, or until potatoes are tender and turning brown on the edges.

2. In a serving bowl, combine Pesto and yogurt and mix well. Add the hot potato mixture and toss to coat. Serve immediately.

Serves 8

4 pounds russet potatoes
2 tablespoons olive oil
1 onion, chopped
3 cloves garlic, minced
½ cup Basil Pesto (Chapter 7)
¼ cup soy yogurt

Pea Sauté

Serves 6

1 tablespoon olive oil
1 shallot, minced
3 cloves garlic, minced
2 cups frozen baby peas
2 cups frozen sugar snap pea
    pods
2 tablespoons water
½ teaspoon salt
Pinch pepper

Who doesn't love peas? This simple side dish takes just minutes to make.

1. In a medium saucepan, heat olive oil over medium heat. Add shallot and garlic; cook and stir for 4–5 minutes, until crisp-tender.

2. Add peas and water; bring to a simmer. Cover and cook, shaking pan occasionally, until peas are hot and tender, about 4–6 minutes. Drain, then sprinkle with salt and pepper. Serve immediately.

Fried Rice

Fried rice is an exciting, restaurant-style dish that doesn't contain lactose, as long as you're careful in your broth selection! If you add some chicken or ham to this easy recipe, you've created a main dish.

1. In a small bowl, combine broth, soy sauce, gingerroot, and pepper; mix well and set aside.

2. In a wok or large skillet, heat olive oil over medium-high heat. Add onion and garlic; stir-fry for 3 minutes. Add carrot and green onion; stir-fry for 2–3 minutes longer.

3. Add rice; stir-fry until rice is hot and grains are separate, about 4–5 minutes. Stir broth mixture and add to wok; stir-fry until hot, about 3–4 minutes. Serve immediately.

Serves 6

¼ cup vegetable broth
1 tablespoon soy sauce
1 tablespoon minced fresh gingerroot
⅛ teaspoon pepper
2 tablespoons olive oil
1 onion, chopped
3 cloves garlic, minced
½ cup shredded carrot
½ cup chopped green onions
4 cups long-grain rice, cooked and cooled

Cooking Rice

If you have trouble cooking rice, get a rice cooker. This inexpensive appliance cooks rice to fluffy perfection every time. Another option is to cook rice like you cook pasta—in a large pot of boiling water. Keep tasting the rice; when it's tender, thoroughly drain and use in a recipe or serve.

Hash Brown Casserole

Serves 8–10

1 (32-ounce) package
   frozen hash brown potatoes,
   thawed
1 onion, minced
2 cloves garlic, minced
1 teaspoon salt
¼ teaspoon white pepper
1 cup lactose-free cream
   cheese
⅓ cup soy or rice milk
2 cups shredded lactose-free
   cheese
Cooking spray, as needed

This recipe makes a huge amount, so it's perfect for entertaining or holidays.

1. Preheat oven to 375°F. Spray a 13" × 9" baking dish with nonstick cooking spray and set aside.

2. In a large bowl, combine all ingredients and mix well. Spoon into a baking dish and spread into an even layer. Cover and bake for 30 minutes, then uncover and bake for 30–40 minutes longer, or until casserole is bubbly and starting to brown. Serve immediately.

Hash Brown Potatoes

You can find hash brown potatoes in the refrigerated and freezer sections of your local grocery store. Read labels to learn which one has the fewest additives and other ingredients. To thaw the frozen potatoes, just let the bag stand in the refrigerator overnight. Drain the potatoes well before using in recipes.

Smashed Potatoes

These rustic potatoes aren't smashed perfectly smooth. The skins are left on, which adds nutrients and fiber.

1. Scrub potatoes and cut into 1" pieces. Bring a large pot of water to a boil. Add potatoes; bring back to a simmer. Simmer for 10–20 minutes, or until potatoes are tender when pierced with a fork. Drain, then return potatoes to hot pot.

2. Meanwhile, in a small saucepan, heat olive oil over medium heat; cook garlic and shallots. Place pot with hot potatoes over medium heat and, using a fork, mash in the garlic mixture. Leave some pieces of the potato whole.

3. Stir in the cream cheese, 2 tablespoons soy milk, salt, and pepper; add enough milk for desired consistency. Serve immediately. Or you can keep these potatoes warm in a double boiler over simmering water for about an hour.

Serves 6

6 Yukon Gold potatoes
3 tablespoons olive oil
3 garlic cloves, minced
2 shallots, minced
1 (3-ounce) package lactose-free cream cheese, softened
2–4 tablespoons soy milk
½ teaspoon salt
⅛ teaspoon pepper

Sparkly Carrots

Serves 4

1 tablespoon olive oil
2 shallots, minced
2 cups baby carrots
½ cup lime carbonated soda
¼ teaspoon salt
⅛ teaspoon pepper

Use your favorite clear carbonated soda in this easy recipe. It adds a slightly sweet crispness to this side dish.

1. In a large skillet, heat olive oil over medium heat. Add shallots; cook and stir until crisp-tender, about 2 minutes. Add carrots; cook and stir for 2–3 minutes.

2. Add soda, salt, and pepper to skillet and bring to a boil. Reduce heat, cover, and simmer for 4–5 minutes, or until carrots are tender. Serve immediately.

Baby Carrots

Baby carrots aren't just ordinary carrots cut down to size. Ordinary carrots have a clear orange center that isn't as sweet as the rest of the carrot. If made from regular carrots, baby carrots would consist of mostly the center. They are made from a special variety of carrot that is cut down to the baby carrot size. They're delicious eaten cooked or raw.

Baked Squash

In the fall, baked squash is a wonderful side dish that you can flavor many ways. Try baking it with onion and hot chili peppers instead of the juices, sugar, and cinnamon!

1. Preheat oven to 375°F. Remove seeds from squash and discard. Place squash in a baking dish large enough to hold the halves snugly, cut side up. Cover tightly with foil; bake for 20 minutes.

2. In a small saucepan, cook onion and garlic in olive oil until tender, about 5 minutes. Remove from heat and stir in juices, brown sugar, cinnamon, salt, and pepper, and mix well. Spoon mixture into squash halves, making sure to baste the flesh with the liquid.

3. Return to the oven and bake, uncovered, for 20–30 minutes longer, or until squash is very tender, basting occasionally with the liquid. Serve immediately.

Serves 4–6

2 acorn squash, cut in half
1 tablespoon olive oil
1 onion, chopped
2 cloves garlic, minced
2 tablespoons lemon juice
2 tablespoons orange juice
1 tablespoon grapefruit juice
2 tablespoons brown sugar
½ teaspoon cinnamon
½ teaspoon salt
⅛ teaspoon pepper

Veggie Risotto

Serves 8

5 cups vegetable broth
2 tablespoons olive oil
1 onion, chopped
2 cloves garlic, minced
1 (8-ounce) package mush-
  rooms, sliced
3 large carrots, sliced
½ teaspoon salt
⅛ teaspoon pepper
½ teaspoon dried thyme
  leaves
2 cups Arborio rice
½ cup dry white wine
1 cup frozen baby peas,
  thawed

Since there's no butter or cheese in this recipe, as there is in classic risotto, you really need to use Arborio rice for the creamiest texture.

1. Place broth in a medium saucepan; heat over low heat. Meanwhile, in a large skillet, heat olive oil over medium heat. Add onion and garlic; cook and stir until crisp-tender, about 4 minutes.

2. Add mushrooms, carrot, salt, pepper, thyme, and rice; cook and stir for 2–3 minutes. Add wine, and stir until absorbed.

3. Slowly add the warm broth, ½ cup at a time, stirring constantly. Add the peas with the last ½ cup of broth. The rice should be tender yet firm in the center, with a creamy sauce. Serve immediately.

Mashed Sweet Potatoes

This is the perfect dish for Thanksgiving dinner. Make it about an hour ahead of time and keep the potatoes warm in a slow cooker.

1. Peel the sweet potatoes and cut into 1" chunks. Place in a large pot full of cold water; add half of the juice. Bring to a boil, then reduce heat, cover, and simmer for 10–20 minutes, or until sweet potatoes are soft.

2. Drain and return to hot pot. Add olive oil and gingerroot; mash using a potato masher. Add remaining pineapple-orange juice along with salt and pepper; stir until combined. Serve immediately or hold on warm in a slow cooker.

Sweet Potato or Yam?

Yams are not commonly sold in the United States; what we see in the market are two varieties of sweet potatoes. There's a pale-skinned variety that is not sweet, and one with an orange skin and flesh that is sweet and moist when cooked. It's the latter type that is used for Thanksgiving side dishes and mashed sweet potatoes.

Serves 6

4 large sweet potatoes
1 (6-ounce) can pineapple-orange juice, divided
2 tablespoons olive oil
1 tablespoon minced fresh gingerroot
½ teaspoon salt
⅛ teaspoon pepper

Baked Rice Pilaf

Serves 6

2 cups chicken stock
½ cup water
2 tablespoons olive oil
1 onion, chopped
½ cup shredded carrots
½ teaspoon salt
⅛ teaspoon pepper
½ teaspoon dried marjoram
    leaves
1¼ cups long-grain white rice

This rendition of rice pilaf has a decidedly different flavor from the earlier recipe. For a vegetarian side dish, use vegetable broth or water instead of the chicken stock.

1. Preheat oven to 350°F. Combine chicken stock and water in a small saucepan and place over medium heat.

2. Meanwhile, heat olive oil in an ovenproof, 2-quart skillet over medium heat. Add onion; cook and stir until crisp-tender, about 4 minutes. Add carrots, salt, pepper, and marjoram; cook and stir for 2 minutes longer.

3. Stir in rice; cook and stir for 3 minutes longer. Pour hot chicken stock mixture over all and stir.

4. Cover and bake for 35–45 minutes, or until rice is tender and liquid is absorbed; fluff with a fork. Serve.

Zucchini Stir-Fry

If you have a garden, you know August and September can mean bumper crops of zucchini and tomatoes. Use the proceeds in this easy side dish recipe.

1. In a wok or large skillet, heat olive oil over medium-high heat. Add zucchini and shallot; stir-fry until crisp-tender, about 5–7 minutes.

2. Add grape tomatoes, salt, pepper, and thyme leaves; stir-fry until hot and all vegetables are tender, about 3–5 minutes longer. Serve immediately.

Serves 4

2 tablespoons olive oil
2 cups sliced zucchini
2 shallots, minced
2 cups grape tomatoes, halved
½ teaspoon salt
⅛ teaspoon pepper
½ teaspoon dried thyme
   leaves

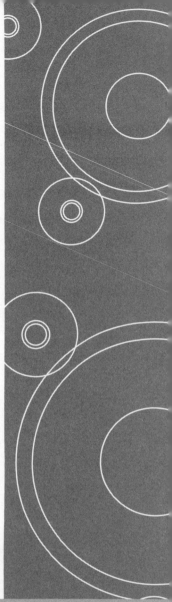

Chicken

chapter eleven

Chicken with Blackberry Mustard

Serves 5

5 (4-ounce) boneless, skinless
  chicken breasts
1 teaspoon paprika
1 teaspoon coarse salt
½ teaspoon ground sage
1 teaspoon pepper
1 tablespoon onion powder
2 tablespoons olive oil
1½ cups blackberry jam
6 tablespoons Dijon mustard
¼ cup chopped fresh parsley

Blackberry mustard is tantalizing to your taste buds! Be sure to check the label on the prepared mustard that you choose to buy for any lurking lactose.

1. Cut chicken breasts into small, 1" cubes. Set aside in refrigerator until ready to use.

2. In a small bowl, combine paprika, salt, sage, pepper, and onion powder to make spice mix. Stir well. Dust chicken cubes with the spice mixture and allow to stand for 15 minutes.

3. Heat the olive oil in a large, heavy skillet over medium heat. Sauté the chicken until done. Set aside and keep warm.

4. Combine blackberry jam and Dijon mustard in the skillet over medium heat. Stir until well combined and warm.

5. Sprinkle chicken with chopped fresh parsley. Serve with blackberry mustard.

Blackberry Bramble

Wild blackberries grow on bramble bushes. These sweet and juicy little berries are high in fiber and pack a powerful antioxidant punch in addition to being a good source of vitamins C and E, iron, and calcium. Add fresh blackberries to your choice of yogurt for a great LI snack!

Spicy Chicken with Mango Sauce

The mango sauce is the star of this dish, and the chili provides a trace of kick.

Serves 2

1 ripe mango
2 tablespoons fresh lemon juice
2 ounces plain soy yogurt
4 leaves leaf lettuce
1 red chili or to taste
8 ounces boneless, skinless chicken breasts
2 tablespoons olive oil
Salt to taste

1. Peel the mango, cutting fruit away from the seed in wide strips. Drizzle mango strips with lemon juice.

2. In a blender, finely purée ⅓ of the mango pieces with the yogurt until well combined and smooth. Cover and place in refrigerator until serving time.

3. Tear lettuce leaves into large pieces. Slit open the chili. Trim and cut into thin rings. Rinse chicken and pat dry with paper towels. Cut into finger-width strips.

4. Heat oil in a nonstick skillet over medium-high heat. Add chicken strips and chili when oil is hot. Sauté on all sides for about 4 minutes until golden brown. Make sure chicken is cooked thoroughly. Season with salt to taste.

5. Arrange the chicken and chili mixture on the lettuce on plates. Garnish with the mango pieces and drizzle with the mango sauce.

Mango Madness

Mangoes are an extremely versatile fruit. You can eat them for breakfast, lunch, dinner, snacks, and desserts—and when they're in season, it may be difficult to resist doing just that! Blend them into a smoothie for breakfast, use them to flavor your salad dressing for lunch, top your dinner with mango salsa, and eat it with a sorbet for dessert.

Oven-Fried Sesame Chicken

Serves 4

3 tablespoons toasted sesame
   seeds
2 tablespoons all-purpose
   flour
¼ teaspoon pepper
2 tablespoons soy sauce
4 (4-ounce) chicken breast
   halves, skinned
2 tablespoons margarine,
   melted

There are healthy ways to satisfy your hunger for fried foods. This oven-fried sesame chicken is sure to please that hankerin' for fried chicken!

1. Preheat oven to 400°F.

2. In a small, flat bowl, combine sesame seeds, flour, and pepper.

3. Pour soy sauce in a saucer. Dip chicken into soy sauce, then dredge in sesame seed mixture.

4. Arrange chicken, bone side down, in a large, shallow baking dish. Melt margarine and drizzle over chicken.

5. Bake for 45 minutes or until chicken is tender.

Lemon Chicken with Broccoli

You just can't beat combining fresh broccoli with freshly squeezed lemon juice. If you're watching your weight, this recipe is great without the rice.

1. Dice chicken into bite-sized pieces. Heat oil in a large, heavy skillet or wok. Stir-fry until chicken is done and no longer pink.

2. Break broccoli into florets and steam until crisp-tender. Add broccoli to chicken.

3. In a small saucepan, stir together salt, sugar, lemon juice, water, and cornstarch. Heat over medium heat, stirring constantly until sauce thickens.

4. Pour sauce over chicken and broccoli. Heat through. Serve over steamed rice.

Serves 4

4 (4-ounce) boneless, skinless chicken breasts
1 tablespoon olive oil
½ pound broccoli crowns
1 teaspoon salt
¼ cup sugar
1½ tablespoons fresh lemon juice
¾ cup water
3 tablespoons cornstarch
2 cups prepared steamed rice (optional)

Grilled Balsamic Chicken

Serves 8

1 (3-pound) chicken, quartered
¼ cup chicken broth
½ cup balsamic vinegar
⅓ cup green onions, chopped
2 tablespoons Dijon mustard
1 tablespoon garlic, minced
1 tablespoon sugar
2 teaspoons Worcestershire sauce
1 teaspoon dry mustard
1 teaspoon cracked black pepper

Balsamic vinegar is sweet yet simultaneously tart. It blends deliciously with chicken.

1. Rinse chicken pieces and pat dry. Arrange chicken in a shallow baking dish.

2. Combine remaining ingredients in a small bowl and whisk to blend well. Pour marinade over chicken. Cover and refrigerate for at least 24 hours, turning occasionally.

3. Preheat oven to 325°F or prepare grill for cooking.

4. Oven instructions: Bring chicken and marinade to room temperature. (Don't let it sit out longer than 1½–2 hours at the most.) Bake for 30–40 minutes or until chicken is done.

5. Grilling instructions: Remove chicken from marinade. Place on grill until chicken is done (this will vary according to size of chicken quarters). Turn chicken only once during grilling.

Pecan Chicken Breasts

Pecans provide a subtle crunch to a naturally soft bird. The texture and the taste blend for a startlingly exciting dish.

1. Mix bread crumbs and pecans in a flat dish. Sprinkle flour in a shallow dish or glass pie plate. Season with salt and pepper.

2. Beat the egg substitute, water, and Tabasco sauce in a medium bowl.

3. Dip chicken breasts first in the flour, then in the egg mixture, then in the bread crumb mixture. Place on a plate. Cover and refrigerate for at least 30 minutes.

4. Coat a large skillet with cooking spray. Melt margarine over medium heat.

5. Add chicken breasts. Cook for about 30 minutes, making sure to brown evenly on all sides.

Pecan Prattle

Pecans are delicious and nutritious! The fat found in pecans contains no cholesterol and is mostly monounsaturated fat (65 percent monounsaturated, 35 percent polyunsaturated). Pecans give you vitamins A, B, and C, plus potassium, phosphorous, iron, and calcium. They are also a good source of protein and fiber—hard to believe a little nut can hold all that nutrition!

Serves 4

1 cup bread crumbs
¼ cup finely chopped pecans
½ cup flour
Salt to taste
¼ teaspoon black pepper
½ cup egg substitute
1 tablespoon water
2 dashes Tabasco sauce or to taste
4 (4-ounce) boneless, skinless chicken breasts
Nonstick cooking spray
2 tablespoons margarine

Paprika Yogurt Chicken

Serves 4

1 tablespoon olive oil
1 onion, finely chopped
1 tablespoon minced fresh
  ginger
2 cloves garlic, minced
2 tablespoons paprika
Salt to taste
Cayenne pepper to taste
Pinch of sugar
½ pound sliced fresh mushrooms
2 tomatoes, coarsely chopped
½ cup plain soy yogurt
1 pound boneless, skinless
  chicken breasts

This dish's unique blend of tastes will please your palate even as your brain struggles to identify all the different flavors. Cooking with soy yogurt allows you to enjoy "creamy" and low lactose all at the same time!

1. Heat olive oil in a heavy 10" skillet.

2. Cook onion, ginger, and garlic together.

3. Add paprika, salt, cayenne pepper, sugar, mushrooms, tomatoes, and yogurt. Cook for about 5 minutes.

4. Add chicken and cook until thoroughly done.

5. Serve immediately.

Berried Chicken

Berry, berry good! This colorful recipe is a fun variation for chicken. With flavors like these, you'll find you don't need to turn to creamy, lactose-heavy dishes for excitement on the plate.

Serves 8

2 tablespoons oil
1 clove minced garlic
2 pounds boneless chicken breast strips
1 teaspoon salt
1 (16-ounce) can whole cranberry sauce
½ cup cider vinegar
Zest and juice of ½ orange
1 large green pepper
½ cup thinly sliced onion
2 tablespoons cornstarch
¾ cup water
1½ tablespoons soy sauce
Cooked rice (optional)

1. Heat oil over medium-high heat in a large skillet or wok. Add garlic and slightly cook, stirring to mingle with hot oil. Remove garlic from skillet. Add chicken, browning on all sides. Sprinkle with salt if desired.

2. Combine cranberry sauce, vinegar, orange zest, and orange juice in a small bowl. Whisk to blend well. Pour over chicken in skillet. Reduce heat to low. Cover and simmer for about 35 minutes or until chicken is fork-tender.

3. Seed and rinse green pepper. Cut in strips, crosswise. Add green pepper and onion to skillet combination.

4. Combine cornstarch, water, and soy sauce in a screw-top jar. Shake until lumps disappear. Add cornstarch mixture to chicken, stirring constantly to combine smoothly.

5. Simmer until mixture is clear and thickened. Cook only until veggies are crisp-tender. Don't overcook! Serve over hot rice if desired.

Basil Orange Chicken

Serves 4

3 tablespoons fresh chopped basil
2 tablespoons balsamic vinegar
⅓ cup orange marmalade
⅔ cup orange juice
1 teaspoon olive oil
¼ teaspoon fresh ginger, minced
½ teaspoon salt
4 boneless, skinless chicken breasts
2 oranges
1½ teaspoons cornstarch

Fresh basil and fresh ginger blended with the balsamic vinegar produce a sweet yet slightly tart flavor in this recipe. Fresh squeezed orange juice is the best thing for this recipe, so if you can take the time to make some, you should!

1. In a medium bowl, combine chopped basil, vinegar, orange marmalade, ⅔ cup of orange juice, oil, ginger, and salt. Whisk until well blended. Pour ⅔ of the mixture into a medium-sized flat glass dish. Set aside remaining orange mixture in bowl.

2. Thoroughly coat chicken breasts in orange mixture by placing in dish and turning several times. Place chicken in dish in refrigerator for at least 30 minutes to marinate. Peel and section oranges. Set aside.

3. Preheat broiler. Place chicken on broiler rack. Spoon orange marinade on top of chicken. Broil about 6–8 inches from heat for 5 minutes. Turn chicken breasts over and spoon on the rest of the orange marinade. Return chicken to broiler and broil for another 5 minutes until chicken is golden. Make sure liquid running from chicken is clear and chicken is completely cooked through.

4. While chicken is broiling, pour basil-orange mixture from bowl into a small saucepan. Bring to a boil over medium heat. Add cornstarch and cook until mixture begins to thicken, stirring constantly. Add orange sections and gently stir to combine with basil-orange sauce.

5. Place each chicken breast on a warmed plate. Spoon sauce over chicken breasts and serve immediately.

Grilled Ranch Chicken

This simple recipe makes chicken that is moist and tender, with a lot of flavor.

1. In a glass baking dish, combine dressing, lemon juice, and pepper and mix well. Add chicken breasts and turn to coat. Cover and marinate in refrigerator for 3–4 hours.

2. Prepare and preheat grill. Remove chicken from marinade. Grill for 6–8 minutes per side, turning once, until chicken reaches internal temperature of 165°F. Discard any remaining marinade.

Serves 4

½ cup lactose-free ranch
   salad dressing
2 tablespoons lemon juice
⅛ teaspoon pepper
4 boneless, skinless chicken
   breasts

Green Chili Chicken

Serves 6

6 boneless, skinless chicken breasts
1 (4-ounce) can chopped green chilies, drained
1 cup frozen corn
2 tomatoes, chopped
2 tablespoons lime juice
¼ cup chopped cilantro
½ teaspoon salt
⅛ teaspoon cayenne pepper
1 teaspoon cumin

Cooking in parchment paper ensures that the chicken will be tender and juicy. Parchment paper also holds in all the flavors.

1. Preheat oven to 375°F. Cut six 12" squares of parchment paper and place on work surface. Place one chicken breast in center of each.

2. In a medium bowl, combine chilies, corn, tomatoes, lime juice, cilantro, salt, pepper, and cumin and mix well. Divide on top of chicken.

3. Fold edges of parchment paper over chicken and crimp to close. Place on a cookie sheet and bake until chicken is cooked and parchment paper is browned, about 25–35 minutes. Serve immediately.

Mustard Chicken Paillards

This simple method of cooking chicken can also be used with pork chops and fish fillets. Cook the paillards under a broiler that's as hot as you can get it. They're thin enough that they'll cook through before the outsides burn.

1. Preheat broiler. Place chicken breasts, smooth side down, between two sheets of waxed paper. Using a meat mallet or rolling pin, gently pound from the center out, until chicken is ¼" thick.

2. Carefully place chicken, smooth side down, on broiler pan. Broil 6 inches from heat for 3 minutes, then turn with a spatula.

3. While chicken is broiling, combine remaining ingredients in a small bowl. Spoon mixture over the chicken after it has been turned. Broil for 2–4 minutes longer, or until mustard mixture has brown spots and chicken is thoroughly cooked. Serve immediately.

Paillards

Paillards (pronounced "pie-yards") are thinly pounded pieces of meat, usually made of boneless chicken, veal, beef, or turkey. The meat is placed between sheets of waxed paper to help protect the flesh while it is pounded, so it won't tear. This method produces tender meat that cooks very quickly.

Serves 4

4 boneless, skinless chicken breasts
3 tablespoons mustard
½ teaspoon dried thyme leaves
¼ cup soy yogurt
1 tablespoon lemon juice

Poached Chicken

Serves 8

1 tablespoon olive oil
1 onion, chopped
3 pounds chicken parts
2 carrots, sliced
3 cups water
½ teaspoon salt
1 bay leaf
½ teaspoon dried marjoram
    leaves
½ cup chopped celery leaves

Poached chicken can be served on its own, diced up into broth or stock, or used in salads and sandwiches. It freezes well, too.

1. In a large soup pot, heat olive oil over medium heat. Add onion; cook and stir until onion starts to turn golden, about 8 minutes. Add chicken, skin side down. Cook until browned, then turn chicken over.

2. Add all remaining ingredients to pot. Bring to a boil, then skim surface. Reduce heat to low, cover, and cook just below a simmer until chicken is thoroughly cooked, about 30–35 minutes. Remove chicken from liquid; let cool. Remove meat from bones; refrigerate or freeze.

3. The stock can be strained, then saved for soup.

Poaching

Poaching is a cooking technique where food is cooked in a liquid at a temperature just below a simmer. The French say that the liquid or broth is "smiling." It's important to carefully regulate the heat so the exterior of the meat doesn't overcook by the time the interior comes to a safe temperature.

Chicken with Penne

This well-flavored dish is quick and easy to make; it only uses five ingredients! If you have mild LI, consider grating some additional cheese over the top of the pasta. You can use soy cheese as well, but the effect won't be quite the same.

1. Bring a large pot of water to a boil. Sprinkle chicken with salt and pepper. In a heavy skillet, heat olive oil; add chicken. Cook and stir for 4–5 minutes, or until chicken is almost cooked.

2. Add tomato sauce to the chicken and bring to a simmer. Reduce heat and simmer while you cook pasta according to package directions.

3. When chicken is thoroughly cooked and pasta is al dente, drain pasta and add to skillet. Remove from heat; gently stir in Pesto. Serve immediately.

Serves 6

4 boneless, skinless chicken breasts, cubed
½ teaspoon salt
⅛ teaspoon pepper
2 tablespoons extra-virgin olive oil
1½ cups jarred tomato sauce
1 (16-ounce) package pasta
½ cup Basil Pesto (Chapter 7)

Grilled Pesto Chicken

Serves 6

6 boneless, skinless chicken
    breasts
2 tablespoons lime juice
1 teaspoon dried basil leaves
½ teaspoon salt
⅛ teaspoon pepper
¼ teaspoon garlic powder
1 tablespoon olive oil
½ cup Basil Pesto (Chapter 7)
¼ cup dairy-free vegan sour
    cream

This simple dish can be served with a fresh salsa instead of the basil mixture if you prefer to cut all lactose from the meal.

1. Place chicken breasts in a large glass dish. Sprinkle with lime juice, basil, salt, pepper, garlic powder, and olive oil; rub to coat. Let stand at room temperature for 30 minutes.

2. Prepare and preheat grill. Meanwhile, in small bowl combine Pesto and sour cream; mix and refrigerate.

3. Grill chicken on oiled rack, turning once, for 10–13 minutes, until chicken is thoroughly cooked with an internal temperature of 165°F. Place chicken on a serving plate and top each with a spoonful of Pesto mixture. Serve with remaining Pesto mixture.

Chicken Risotto

This risotto is as creamy as can be, despite not using any dairy! It will fool everyone at your table, since the starch that comes off of the rice will thicken the sauce to a creamy consistency. Make sure to stir the risotto frequently as you cook it!

1. Place stock in a medium saucepan and place on stove over low heat. Cut chicken into 1" pieces and sprinkle with salt and pepper. Heat olive oil in a large heavy saucepan. Add chicken; cook and stir until almost cooked through, about 5–6 minutes. Remove chicken from pan and set aside.

2. Add onion and mushrooms to drippings remaining in saucepan; cook and stir until crisp-tender, about 4 minutes. Add rice and thyme leaves; cook and stir for 2–3 minutes longer.

3. Add wine or stock; cook and stir until liquid is absorbed, about 5 minutes. Add warm stock, ½ cup at a time, stirring after each addition, until rice absorbs liquid.

4. When you have added 3 cups of stock, return chicken to saucepan. Continue adding stock, stirring frequently, until liquid is absorbed.

5. When the mixture is creamy and rice is done, but still has a bit of texture to the center, remove from heat and serve immediately.

Mushrooms

Surprisingly, since they grow in the dark, mushrooms are a good source of vitamin D. To prepare them, don't rinse or wash them or they will become tough. They grow in sterile soil, so just wipe them with a damp paper towel or mushroom brush. Cut off the bottoms of the stems and discard because they can be tough, then slice or chop.

Serves 6

5 cups chicken stock
3 boneless, skinless chicken breasts
½ teaspoon salt
⅛ teaspoon white pepper
3 tablespoons olive oil
1 onion, chopped
1 (8-ounce) package mushrooms, chopped
1½ cups long-grain rice
½ teaspoon dried thyme leaves
½ cup dry white wine, or more stock

Chicken Fried Rice

Serves 4

1 tablespoon olive oil
1 onion, chopped
2 cloves garlic, minced
1 tablespoon grated gingerroot
2 cups cold, cooked rice
1 cup frozen baby peas
2 cups chopped Poached
    Chicken (this chapter)
2 tablespoons low-sodium soy
    sauce
3 tablespoons chicken stock
½ teaspoon dried thyme
    leaves
⅛ teaspoon white pepper

Have everything ready before you start stir-frying, as the process is very quick. All the ingredients have to be prepared ahead of time.

1. Heat olive oil in a large skillet. Add onion and garlic; stir-fry for 4–5 minutes, until crisp-tender. Add ginger, rice, and peas; stir-fry for 3–4 minutes longer.

2. Add chicken; stir-fry until chicken is hot, about 3–5 minutes longer. Stir in soy sauce, stock, thyme, and pepper. Stir-fry until rice absorbs the liquid and food is hot, about 3–4 minutes. Serve immediately.

Chicken Paillards with Zucchini

This simple chicken dish is healthy and beautiful, too. Serve with a green salad drizzled with homemade dressing.

1. Place chicken, smooth side down, between sheets of plastic wrap. Using a rolling pin or meat mallet, pound chicken until about ⅓" thick. Remove plastic wrap; sprinkle chicken with cornstarch, salt, pepper, and thyme.

2. In a large saucepan, heat olive oil over medium-high heat. Add chicken; cook, turning once, until cooked through, about 4–5 minutes per side. Remove chicken from pan and keep warm.

3. Add onion to saucepan; cook and stir until crisp-tender, about 4 minutes. Add zucchini; cook and stir for 4 minutes longer. Return chicken to pan and add basil, stock, and grape tomatoes. Bring to a simmer; cook for 2–3 minutes. Serve immediately.

Zucchini

Zucchini is a mild vegetable with high water and fiber contents. It is delicious eaten raw with appetizer dips and on sandwiches, and good in stir-fries and soups. Look for smaller zucchini with tender skin and those that are heavy for their size. Zucchini will keep in the refrigerator for 3–4 days after purchase.

Serves 4

4 boneless, skinless chicken breasts
2 tablespoons cornstarch
½ teaspoon salt
⅛ teaspoon pepper
½ teaspoon dried thyme leaves
2 tablespoons olive oil
1 onion, chopped
1 zucchini, sliced
3 tablespoons torn fresh basil leaves
¼ cup chicken stock
2 cups grape tomatoes

Beef

chapter twelve

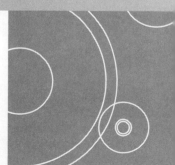

Sizzling Beef Teriyaki

Serves 4

1 pound beef round steak
¼ cup soy sauce
1 tablespoon dry sherry
1 tablespoon sugar
½ teaspoon grated fresh
    ginger
¼ teaspoon garlic powder
Cooked rice (optional)

A good beef teriyaki recipe can be used in a variety of ways and doesn't always have to be served over rice. Toss the beef with a variety of freshly steamed veggies.

1. Cut slightly frozen beef into ⅛"-thick strips.

2. In a medium bowl, mix soy sauce, sherry, sugar, ginger, and garlic powder. Stir in meat. Allow to marinate for 15 minutes.

3. Thread beef on skewers. Preheat broiler or prepare grill.

4. Broil 4 inches from heat for 2 minutes on each side or until done as desired. Serve on hot cooked rice.

Rice Spells "Variety"!

There are so many different varieties of rice. Be experimental with your rice choices. Read the labels and familiarize yourself with the nutritional values of rice, then take them home and cook with them to see which ones you like the best.

Beef Stroganoff

Serve this to guests and they'll think they're dining in a fine restaurant instead of your home! Be sure to use "unsweetened" soy milk for this recipe or substitute your favorite lactose-free milk.

1. In a small bowl, combine soy milk and vinegar. Allow to stand for 15 minutes. Meanwhile, cut beef across grain into thin slices.

2. In a large skillet, heat 1 tablespoon oil over high heat. Add beef. Stir-fry for 1 minute. Remove beef from skillet.

3. Add remaining 2 tablespoons oil to skillet and heat. Add onion and mushrooms. Stir-fry for 4 minutes. Reduce heat to medium.

4. In a small bowl, blend flour, soy sauce, garlic, and ¼ cup water. Add to skillet, stirring constantly. Bring to a boil. Stir constantly and cook for 1 minute.

5. Gradually add soy milk mixture. Add beef and parsley, continuing to stir constantly. Cook until just heated through. Serve over cooked noodles.

Serves 4

1 cup unsweetened soy milk
1 tablespoon white vinegar
1 pound boneless tender beef steak
3 tablespoons olive oil
1 small onion, thinly sliced
½ pound fresh mushrooms, sliced
2½ tablespoons all-purpose flour
¼ cup soy sauce
1 clove garlic, pressed
¼ cup water
⅓ cup minced fresh parsley
Wide egg noodles, cooked

Curry Slurry

Serves 6

Nonstick cooking spray
3 tablespoons margarine
1 large yellow onion, finely
chopped
1 pound lean ground beef
1 tablespoon curry powder (or
to taste)
2 Roma tomatoes, cut in
chunks
1 (9-ounce) can peas, undrained
½ teaspoon chili powder
1 teaspoon paprika
1 teaspoon salt
Cooked rice (optional)

It's up to you how highly seasoned you want this dish to be. If you're a curry fan, go for it—it's totally lactose-free!

1. Spray a large skillet with cooking spray. Heat margarine in skillet over medium-high heat.

2. Sauté onion and push to one side of skillet.

3. Shape ground beef into a large patty. Brown for about 5 minutes on each side. Break meat into chunks.

4. Add all remaining ingredients to meat and onion mixture. Reduce heat and simmer for 30 minutes.

5. Serve over cooked rice if desired.

Old-Fashioned Meatloaf

Meatloaf is good for a hot entrée, and it makes great sandwiches the next day. In fact, some say the true test of meatloaf is whether it makes good sandwiches! Just remember to read labels on your store-bought condiment ingredients to check for any nasty lactose lurkers that will make your tummy not like the meatloaf.

1. Preheat oven to 350°F.

2. Combine all ingredients except the tomato sauce. Thoroughly mix with your hands. Shape into a loaf.

3. Place in a 9" × 5" pan. Spoon tomato sauce over top of loaf.

4. Bake for 1 hour. Drain fat and juices.

5. Let stand for 5 minutes before slicing and serving.

Leaner Than Lean

Do you know what those "lean" labels on ground beef really mean? Let's say you need one pound of ground beef. If the label reads that the ground beef is 95 percent lean, it has 23 grams of fat (before cooking). Compare that to one pound of ground beef that is 80 percent lean, which has 91 grams of fat.

Serves 6

1½ pounds extra-lean ground beef
½ cup chopped onion
¼ green pepper, finely chopped
¾ cup oatmeal, quick or old-fashioned
¼ cup egg substitute
1 tablespoon prepared horse-radish
1 teaspoon dry mustard
¼ cup ketchup
¼ cup tomato juice
1 teaspoon Worcestershire sauce
½ teaspoon salt (optional)
¼ teaspoon pepper
1 cup tomato sauce

Meatballs and Sauerkraut

Serves 6

1½ pounds lean ground beef
Salt and pepper to taste
1 cup diced onions
4 cups tomato juice
2 (1-pound) cans sauerkraut
1 tablespoon fresh lemon juice
1 teaspoon sugar

This easy recipe is sure to be a hit at your next party. Use your slow cooker instead of stovetop cooking, and set it on the table for serving.

1. Preheat oven to 350°F. Place ground beef in a medium bowl. Add salt and pepper to taste.

2. Shape meat into balls about the size of large walnuts. Place in a shallow baking pan on middle rack in oven. Bake for 30 minutes, uncovered, until meatballs are nicely browned.

3. Sprinkle onions in the bottom of a large saucepan. Add ½ cup of tomato juice. Cook over low heat until onions are tender. Add more tomato juice if necessary.

4. Begin layering meatballs and sauerkraut on top of onion and tomato mixture, beginning with meatballs. Alternate layers.

5. Add lemon juice and sugar to tomato juice. Stir to blend. Pour over meatballs and sauerkraut. Reduce heat to low; cover and simmer for 1 hour.

Sauerkraut's in a Pickle!

Sauerkraut only has 20 calories per half-cup serving. It also provides iron, vitamins C and B, potassium, calcium, and fiber. But beware of the sodium content. Read the labels. To reduce the sodium content, drain, rinse, and drain sauerkraut again before using.

Savory Grilled Steaks

Marinating steaks adds to their flavor and helps tenderize the meat by breaking down fibers with acidic ingredients.

1. In a large zip-top, heavy-duty food storage bag, combine all ingredients except steaks; seal and knead to blend. Add steaks and turn to coat. Place bag in a glass bowl; refrigerate for 3–4 hours.

2. When ready to eat, prepare and preheat grill. Remove steaks from marinade; discard marinade. Grill steaks 6 inches from medium coals for 4–8 minutes on each side, until food thermometer registers at least 145°F, turning once.

3. Remove steaks from grill and cover with foil. Let stand for 5–10 minutes before serving.

Serves 6

2 garlic cloves, minced
2 tablespoons tomato paste
1 tablespoon olive oil
3 tablespoons balsamic
  vinegar
¼ teaspoon pepper
1 tablespoon soy sauce
6 (6-ounce) sirloin steaks

Beef Piccata

Piccata is usually made with chicken or veal, but beef is a nice twist on a classic.

Serves 4

4 (6-ounce) top round steaks
3 tablespoons rice milk
2 tablespoons potato-starch flour
2 tablespoons cornstarch
½ teaspoon pepper
½ teaspoon salt
½ teaspoon paprika
2 tablespoons olive oil
1 (8-ounce) package mushrooms, sliced
3 cloves garlic, minced
1 cup beef stock
¼ cup dry red wine, if desired
3 tablespoons water
1 tablespoon cornstarch

1. Place beef between sheets of waxed paper and pound gently with meat mallet or rolling pin to slightly flatten. Place rice milk in a shallow bowl. In another shallow bowl, combine potato-starch flour, cornstarch, pepper, salt, and paprika.

2. Dip beef into milk, then into flour mixture to coat. In a large saucepan, heat olive oil over medium-high heat. Add beef; brown on both sides, turning once, about 5–6 minutes. Remove from pan.

3. Add mushrooms and garlic to pan; cook and stir until tender, about 5–6 minutes. Add stock and wine and bring to a simmer. Return steaks to pan; simmer for 15–25 minutes, or until beef is tender.

4. In a small bowl, combine water and cornstarch and mix well. Add to saucepan; cook and stir until sauce is slightly thickened. Serve immediately.

Taco Pasta

This hearty and flavorful dish can be made spicier if you add more jalapeño peppers or chili powder. Season to taste!

1. Bring a large pot of water to a boil. In a large saucepan, cook ground beef with onion and garlic, stirring to break up meat, until beef is browned. Drain thoroughly. Add bell pepper and jalapeño peppers to saucepan; cook and stir for 1 minute longer.

2. Add tomatoes, tomato sauce, tomato juice, and taco seasoning to the saucepan; stir to combine. Bring to a boil, reduce heat to low, and simmer for 15–20 minutes.

3. When sauce is almost cooked, cook spaghetti in the water according to package directions until al dente. Drain well and place on a serving plate. Top with beef mixture. Sprinkle with corn chips and cheese; serve with sour cream.

Make It Spicy

For spicier foods, use habanero or Scotch Bonnet peppers instead of jalapeños. The smaller the pepper, the more heat it has. The heat of the pepper, called capsaicin, is mostly contained in the membranes and seeds of the peppers. For a milder taste, remove the membranes and seeds before chopping or mincing.

Serves 6–8

1 pound ground beef
1 onion, chopped
4 cloves garlic, minced
1 green bell pepper, chopped
1–2 jalapeño peppers, minced
1 (14-ounce) can diced tomatoes, undrained
1 (8-ounce) can tomato sauce
½ cup tomato juice
2 tablespoons taco seasoning
1 (12-ounce) package spaghetti
½ cup crushed corn chips
½ cup shredded lactose-free cheese
½ cup lactose-free sour cream

Marinated Flank Steak

Serves 4

⅓ cup dry red wine
2 tablespoons brown sugar
1 tablespoon honey
2 tablespoons beef stock
2 cloves garlic, minced
1 onion, minced
1 jalapeño pepper, minced, if
  desired
⅛ teaspoon pepper
½ teaspoon salt
1½ pounds flank steak

Flank steak is tender, juicy, and succulent when marinated and cooked until medium or medium-well.

1. In a large zip-top food storage bag, combine all ingredients except flank steak. Add steak, seal bag, and knead bag gently to mix.

2. Place bag in a large pan and refrigerate for 18–24 hours, turning bag occasionally.

3. When ready to eat, prepare and preheat grill. Remove steak from marinade; discard marinade. Grill steak 6 inches from medium coals for 12–16 minutes, turning once, until desired doneness. Cover and let stand for 5 minutes. Slice across grain to serve.

Flank Steak

Flank steak has a clearly defined grain running through the meat. This looks like fine lines in the flesh. When you cut flank steak, whether you're cutting it before cooking or after, it must be cut against the grain. That means you should make your cuts perpendicular to the lines in the meat.

Asian Steaks

Asian flavors infuse this tender steak. Serve it with some fried rice, a napa cabbage salad, and fresh fruit for dessert. The strong flavors of the five-spice powder, rice wine vinegar, and garlic are sure to perk up your tastebuds.

1. In a large zip-top food storage bag, combine all ingredients except flank steak. Add steak, seal bag, and knead bag gently to mix.

2. Place bag in a large pan and refrigerate for 18–24 hours, turning bag occasionally.

3. When ready to eat, prepare and preheat grill. Remove steak from marinade; discard marinade. Grill steak 6 inches from medium coals for 12–16 minutes, turning once, until desired doneness. Cover and let stand for 5 minutes, then slice across the grain to serve.

Serves 4

1 tablespoon minced ginger-root
2 cloves garlic, minced
1 shallot, minced
½ teaspoon five-spice powder
2 tablespoons rice wine vinegar
1 tablespoon lime juice
2 teaspoons soy sauce
2 tablespoons vegetable oil
⅛ teaspoon cayenne pepper
1 pound flank steak

Beef and Pea Stir-Fry

Serves 4

1 pound boneless beef sirloin
   tip steak
⅓ cup beef stock
1 teaspoon sugar
2 tablespoons cornstarch
2 tablespoons apple juice
2 tablespoons soy sauce
⅛ teaspoon pepper
2 tablespoons olive oil
1 onion, sliced
2 cloves garlic, minced
2 cups snow peas
1 cup frozen baby peas

Two kinds of peas make this stir-fry special. Serve with hot cooked rice and a salad made with lettuce and mandarin oranges.

1. Cut beef into ¼" × 4" strips against the grain. In a medium bowl, combine stock, sugar, cornstarch, apple juice, soy sauce, and pepper; mix well. Add beef and let stand for 15 minutes.

2. Drain beef, reserving marinade. Heat olive oil in a wok or large skillet over medium-high heat. Add beef; stir-fry until browned, about 3–4 minutes. Remove beef from wok and set aside.

3. Add onion and garlic to wok; stir-fry for 4–5 minutes until crisp-tender. Add snow peas and baby peas to wok; stir-fry for 2 minutes.

4. Stir marinade and add to wok along with beef. Stir-fry until sauce bubbles and thickens, about 4–5 minutes. Serve immediately over hot cooked rice.

Spaghetti Bolognese

Spaghetti Bolognese is a rich and thick meat sauce well-flavored with onion and herbs. Traditionally, this sauce is bound with cream, but here, it's thickened with beef stock and red wine for a delightfully fresh lactose-free take on a classic.

1. In a large skillet, cook ground beef over medium heat, stirring to break up meat, until partially cooked. Drain beef. Add onions and garlic; continue cooking until beef is browned.

2. Add bell pepper, tomatoes, and canned tomatoes; cook and stir for 5 minutes. In a small bowl, combine stock, wine, and tomato paste; stir with wire whisk until tomato paste dissolves.

3. Add to skillet with bay leaf, sugar, salt, pepper, oregano, and basil; bring to a simmer. Lower heat and simmer for 15–20 minutes.

4. Bring a large pot of water to a boil. Cook pasta until al dente, then drain, reserving ⅓ cup pasta cooking water. Stir pasta into meat sauce along with water, if necessary, if sauce is too thick. Remove and discard bay leaf, top with cheese, and serve immediately.

Spaghetti Bolognese

This dish is very popular in Europe, especially the Scandinavian countries and England. It's traditionally made from prosciutto, beef, carrots, onions, celery, wine, and milk, but different variations abound. You can make your own version by adding bacon or prosciutto, using celery instead of bell pepper, and changing the herbs.

Serves 6–8

1½ pounds lean ground beef
2 onions, chopped
4 cloves garlic, minced
1 green bell pepper, chopped
6 plum tomatoes, chopped
1 (14-ounce) can diced tomatoes, undrained
1 cup beef stock
½ cup red wine
1 (6-ounce) can tomato paste
1 bay leaf
1 teaspoon sugar
½ teaspoon salt
⅛ teaspoon pepper
½ teaspoon dried oregano leaves
½ teaspoon dried basil leaves
1 (16-ounce) package spaghetti
½ cup grated dairy-free, vegan Parmesan cheese

Beef and Bean Enchiladas

Serves 8

1 pound lean ground beef
1 onion, chopped
2 cloves garlic, minced
3 tablespoons taco seasoning
½ cup tomato juice
1 (8-ounce) can tomato sauce
¼ cup tomato paste
1 cup dairy-free vegan sour cream
1 (4-ounce) can green chilies, drained
3 cups shredded lactose-free cheese, divided
12 (6-inch) corn tortillas
1 (15-ounce) can vegetarian refried beans

Enchiladas are spicy and rich, with a wonderful combination of flavors. You can make this casserole ahead of time and refrigerate, baking it for 10–15 minutes longer.

1. Preheat oven to 375°F. In a large skillet, cook ground beef with onion and garlic until beef is browned, stirring to break up meat. Drain well, then stir in taco seasoning, tomato juice, tomato sauce, and tomato paste. Cook, stirring occasionally, until sauce bubbles and thickens, about 10 minutes.

2. In a small bowl, combine sour cream, chilies, and 1 cup of the cheese; mix well.

3. Spread ½ cup of meat sauce in bottom of a 13" × 9" glass baking dish. Arrange tortillas on work surface. Divide refried beans among the tortillas, then top with a spoonful of meat sauce and a spoonful of sour cream mixture.

4. Roll up and place, seam side down, in prepared dish. Pour remaining meat sauce over all, then top with remaining cheese. Bake for 30–40 minutes, or until casserole is bubbling and cheese melts and begins to brown.

Lean Beef Stroganoff

This rich recipe is wonderful for entertaining. Serve with a spinach and pea salad and some garlic bread made with French Bread (Chapter 4).

1. Bring a large pot of water to a boil. Meanwhile, in a small saucepan heat 2 tablespoons olive oil over medium heat. Add potato-starch flour; cook and stir with a wire whisk until bubbly. Add rice milk, stock, and lemon juice and bring to a simmer. Reduce heat to low and simmer for 5 minutes, stirring frequently, until thick. Set aside.

2. Cut steak into ¼" × 4" strips. Toss with 1 tablespoon flour, salt, and pepper. In a large skillet, heat 1 tablespoon olive oil over medium heat. Add steak; brown, stirring occasionally, for 4–5 minutes. Add onion, garlic, mushrooms, and thyme; cook and stir for 5–6 minutes.

3. Cook egg noodles as directed on package until al dente. Add stock mixture and mustard to steak mixture in skillet; simmer for 5–6 minutes to blend flavors. When noodles are cooked, drain and add to skillet. Stir to coat noodles. Serve immediately.

Serves 6

2 tablespoons olive oil
2 tablespoons potato-starch flour
½ cup rice milk
1 cup beef stock
1 tablespoon lemon juice
1 pound sirloin steak
1 tablespoon all-purpose flour
½ teaspoon salt
⅛ teaspoon pepper
1 tablespoon olive oil
1 onion, chopped
3 cloves garlic, minced
1 (8-ounce) package sliced mushrooms
½ teaspoon dried thyme leaves
1 (12-ounce) package rice noodles
1 tablespoon Dijon mustard

Pork and Lamb

chapter thirteen

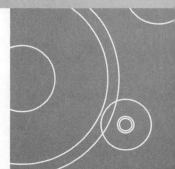

Sausage and Broccoli Stir-Fry

Serves 4

⅛ teaspoon crushed red pep-
    per flakes
1 tablespoon soy sauce
2 tablespoons cornstarch or
    potato-starch flour
¼ teaspoon ginger
½ cup water
1 pound spicy ground pork
    sausage
1 onion, chopped
1 cup sliced fresh mushrooms
2 cups fresh broccoli florets
1 red bell pepper, sliced

Stir-frying is a very quick cooking technique that preserves vitamins and minerals. You don't need a wok to stir-fry, but you do need a very sturdy spatula.

1. In a small bowl, combine red pepper flakes, soy sauce, cornstarch or potato-starch flour, ginger, and water; mix well and set aside.

2. In a large wok or skillet, stir-fry pork sausage with onion until sausage is browned, stirring to break up meat. Remove meat and onions from wok, leaving about 1 tablespoon of drippings.

3. Add mushrooms, broccoli, and bell pepper to wok; stir-fry until crisp-tender, about 4–5 minutes. Stir cornstarch mixture and add to wok along with sausage and onions. Stir-fry until sauce thickens and boils, about 2–3 minutes. Serve immediately over hot cooked rice.

Spaghetti with Ham Sauce

This is the same basic formula used for spaghetti with clam sauce, but it's a novel approach that uses ham instead. If you'd like, you can replace the ham with shaved chunks of prosciutto for a more intensely-flavored dish.

1. Bring a large pot of salted water to a boil. Meanwhile, in a large saucepan, heat olive oil over medium heat. Add onion and garlic; cook and stir until tender, about 6–7 minutes.

2. Sprinkle with salt, pepper, and basil leaves. Add ham and chicken stock; bring to a simmer.

3. Cook pasta according to package directions until almost al dente. Drain and add to saucepan with ham mixture. Cook and stir for 2–3 minutes, until pasta is al dente. Sprinkle with parsley and serve immediately.

Flavored Oils

Flavored oils are a good way to add flavor with fewer ingredients. But please don't make your own. The combination of an anaerobic environment (the oil) with ingredients that can contain bacteria and spores (herbs and garlic) can result in botulism. There are many commercially produced flavored oils to choose from, including basil, garlic, and onion.

Serves 6

2 tablespoons garlic olive oil
2 onions, chopped
4 cloves garlic, minced
½ teaspoon salt
¼ teaspoon pepper
1 teaspoon dried basil leaves
2 cups cubed ham
1 cup chicken stock
1 (16-ounce) package spaghetti
½ cup chopped flat-leaf parsley

Chimichangas

Serves 6–8

1 pound spicy ground pork
    sausage
1 onion, chopped
3 cloves garlic, minced
1 jalapeño pepper, minced
1 green bell pepper, chopped
1 (15-ounce) can refried
    beans
1 (6-ounce) can tomato paste
1 tablespoon chili powder
¼ teaspoon salt
¼ teaspoon white pepper
12 (6-inch) corn tortillas
1½ cups shredded lactose-
    free cheese
2 tablespoons vegetable oil
Salsa
Avocado

Chimichangas are usually deep-fried, but this baked version is easier, and better for you, too.

1. Preheat oven to 375°F. In a large saucepan, cook sausage with onion and garlic, stirring to break up meat. Drain well. Return pan to heat. Add jalapeño and green bell pepper; cook and stir for 3 minutes.

2. Add refried beans, tomato paste, chili powder, salt, and pepper and mix well. Bring to a simmer; simmer, stirring frequently, for 10 minutes.

3. Arrange tortillas on work surface. Place about ¼ cup sausage mixture on each, then top with cheese. Roll up and place seam-side down on a cookie sheet. Repeat with remaining tortillas, cheese, and filling.

4. Brush Chimichangas with oil and bake for 25–35 minutes, or until tortillas are crisp and cheese is melted. Serve immediately with salsa and avocado.

Tortilla Stack

Crisp tortillas are layered with a rich bean and sausage mixture, then baked with lactose-free cheese. Yum!

1. In a large saucepan, cook pork sausage over medium heat, stirring to break up meat, until browned. Drain well. Add red bell pepper; cook and stir for 3 minutes longer. Add chilies, beans, taco seasoning, and tomato sauce and bring to a simmer. Simmer, stirring frequently, for 10 minutes.

2. In another large saucepan, heat vegetable oil over medium-high heat. Fry the tortillas, one at a time, until crisp, turning once, about 2–3 minutes. Drain on paper towels.

3. On a large cookie sheet with sides, place one tortilla. Top with ⅙ of the pork mixture and ⅙ of the cheese. Repeat layers, using 3 tortillas, ending with tortilla and cheese. Repeat with remaining tortillas, pork mixture, and cheese, making three stacks.

4. Bake for 25–35 minutes, or until cheese is melted and bubbly. Let stand for 5 minutes. Cut each stack in thirds to serve.

Serves 6–8

1 pound ground pork sausage
1 red bell pepper, chopped
1 (4-ounce) can chopped green chilies, drained
2 (15-ounce) cans kidney beans, drained
2 tablespoons taco seasoning
1 (8-ounce) can tomato sauce
3 tablespoons vegetable oil
9 (6-inch) corn tortillas
1½ cups shredded lactose-free cheese

Grilled Pork Tenderloin

Serves 6

¼ cup honey
⅓ cup apple jelly
2 tablespoons Dijon mustard
¼ cup chicken stock
½ teaspoon salt
⅛ teaspoon pepper
½ teaspoon dried marjoram
   leaves
2 (1-pound) pork tenderloins

This simple yet flavorful recipe is a good choice for an outdoor cookout. Serve with fresh fruit and potato salad.

1. Combine honey, jelly, mustard, stock, salt, pepper, and marjoram in a small saucepan. Heat over low heat until jelly melts and mixture is blended.

2. Place tenderloins in a glass dish and pour marinade over. Cover and refrigerate for 4–6 hours.

3. When ready to eat, prepare and preheat grill. Drain pork, reserving marinade. Place pork on grill 6 inches from medium coals; cover and grill for 15 minutes.

4. Brush pork with marinade as it grills for another 15–25 minutes, turning occasionally, or until an instant-read meat thermometer registers 155°F. Let pork stand, covered, for 5 minutes before slicing. Discard remaining marinade.

Spicy Grilled Pork Chops

Spicy, tender, juicy, and savory pork chops are a real treat. Serve these with potato salad and a fruit pie for dessert.

1. In a heavy-duty, plastic food storage bag, combine all ingredients except the chops; mix well. Add chops, seal bag, place in a bowl, and refrigerate for 3–4 hours.

2. When ready to eat, prepare and preheat grill. Drain chops, reserving marinade. Grill chops 6 inches from medium coals for 10–12 minutes, basting occasionally with reserved marinade, until meat thermometer registers 155°F. Discard remaining marinade. Serve immediately.

Serves 4

1 tablespoon olive oil
2 cloves garlic, minced
1 jalapeño pepper, minced
1 tablespoon chili powder
2 tablespoons apple cider vinegar
¼ teaspoon salt
⅛ teaspoon pepper
¼ cup pineapple juice
2 tablespoons sugar
⅛ teaspoon cayenne pepper
4 boneless loin pork chops

Sausage Risotto

Serves 6

3 cups chicken stock
1 pound spicy Italian pork
 sausage
1 onion, chopped
1 cup Arborio rice
1 tablespoon fresh chopped
 sage leaves
¼ cup shredded lactose-free
 cheese

This simple dish can be ready in about half an hour, even though you have to stir and stir!

1. Place stock in a small saucepan over low heat. In a large saucepan, cook sausage and onion over medium heat until browned, stirring to break up meat. When pork is cooked, drain, leaving a few spoonfuls of liquid in saucepan.

2. Add rice; cook and stir until rice turns light gold. Add the stock, ½ cup at a time, stirring constantly, until rice is al dente. This should take about 20 minutes.

3. Stir in sage leaves and cheese; cover, remove from heat, and let stand for 5 minutes before serving.

Ham Hash

Make this delicious hash with leftovers from Easter or Christmas dinner. Top each serving with a crisp fried egg for true decadence!

1. In a large skillet, heat oil over medium heat. Add garlic, onion, and potatoes; cook and stir until potatoes start to brown, about 7–8 minutes. Add stock and bring to a simmer. Cover and simmer for 5–6 minutes, until potatoes are almost tender.

2. Add ham, lemon juice, mustard, salt, and pepper. Cook and stir for another 6–8 minutes, stirring frequently, until potatoes are tender. Serve immediately.

Cooking Potatoes

When cooking potatoes in a skillet, stir just enough so the potatoes don't stick, but don't stir too much or they will start to break up. In hash and other casseroles, you do want some brown bits on the potatoes. Leave the skin on, because this adds nutrients and fiber to the finished dish.

Serves 4

1 tablespoon vegetable oil
2 cloves garlic, minced
1 onion, diced
3 russet potatoes, diced
⅓ cup chicken stock
2 cups diced ham
1 tablespoon lemon juice
1 tablespoon mustard
¼ teaspoon salt
⅛ teaspoon pepper

Roasted Apricot Pork Tenderloin

Serves 6

¼ cup apricot preserves
¼ cup apricot nectar
2 tablespoons brown sugar
2 tablespoons apple cider vinegar
2 tablespoons chicken stock
3 cloves garlic, minced
2 pounds pork tenderloin

Pork tenderloin is, as the name says, tender and juicy. It's a very low-fat cut of pork that is easy to prepare and serve.

1. Combine all ingredients except tenderloin in a small bowl. Place pork in a glass baking dish and pour apricot mixture over all. Cover and refrigerate for 8–24 hours.

2. When ready to eat, preheat oven to 325°F. Roast pork with marinade for 40–50 minutes, basting occasionally with marinade, until meat thermometer registers 155°F. Cover pork and let stand for 5 minutes. Slice to serve.

Roasted Pork Tenderloin

Pork tenderloin is low-fat and tender, and is one of the easiest cuts of pork to prepare.

1. Combine all ingredients except pork in a small bowl and mix until blended. Place pork in a 13" × 9" glass baking dish and pour wine mixture over. Cover and refrigerate for 30–40 minutes, turning pork occasionally.

2. When ready to eat, preheat oven to 325°F. Add ¼ cup water to dish with pork and bake for 40–50 minutes, basting occasionally with juices, or until meat thermometer inserted into pork registers 155°F. Let stand for 10 minutes. Slice to serve.

Serves 6

¼ cup red wine
1 shallot, minced
2 cloves garlic, minced
2 tablespoons sugar
1 tablespoon mustard
½ teaspoon salt
⅛ teaspoon pepper
½ teaspoon dried marjoram leaves
2 pounds pork tenderloin

Ham Risotto

Serves 4

4 cups chicken stock
2 tablespoons olive oil
1 onion, chopped
2 cloves garlic, minced
¼ teaspoon salt
⅛ teaspoon white pepper
½ teaspoon dried thyme
    leaves
1 cup chopped ham
1 cup Arborio rice
3 tablespoons pineapple juice
¼ cup grated dairy-free, vegan
    Parmesan cheese

Risotto is a classic Italian dish that isn't difficult to make, but it does take time. Serve this with a fresh green salad and some Seasoned Breadsticks (Chapter 4).

1. In a medium saucepan, place chicken stock over low heat. Meanwhile, in a large saucepan, heat olive oil over medium heat. Add onion and garlic; cook and stir until crisp-tender, about 4 minutes. Sprinkle with salt, pepper, and thyme.

2. Add ham and rice; cook and stir for 3 minutes. Add warm stock, ½ cup at a time, stirring constantly, until liquid is absorbed. Continue adding stock, cooking and stirring, for about 20 minutes.

3. Add the pineapple juice with the last ½ cup of stock; cook and stir until sauce is very creamy and rice is al dente. Stir in cheese. Serve immediately.

Versatile Risotto

Risotto can be made with any meat, or with no meat at all. The only rules are to toast the rice in the fat before the liquid is added, to keep the liquid warm while the risotto is cooking, and to stir pretty much constantly. And make sure to add the cheese at the very end of the cooking time.

Skillet Chops and Veggies

This easy one-dish meal is pure comfort food. Serve with a butter lettuce salad mixed with mushrooms and green peppers.

1. Sprinkle chops with flour, salt, and pepper; set aside. In a large skillet, heat olive oil over medium heat. Add chops; brown for 2–3 minutes on each side. Remove from heat and set aside.

2. Add onion and garlic to skillet; cook and stir until crisp-tender, about 5 minutes. Add potatoes to pan; cook and stir until potatoes are coated. Top with carrots, then add browned pork chops.

3. Add stock and lemon juice and bring to a simmer. Cover skillet tightly, reduce heat to medium-low, and simmer for 35–45 minutes, or until potatoes are tender and chops are cooked, shaking pan occasionally. Serve immediately.

Serves 4

4 (4-ounce) boneless loin pork chops
2 tablespoons potato-starch flour
½ teaspoon salt
⅛ teaspoon pepper
2 tablespoons olive oil
1 onion, chopped
3 cloves garlic, minced
4 russet potatoes, thinly sliced
3 carrots, sliced
1 cup chicken stock
1 tablespoon lemon juice

Herbed Lamb Chops

Serves 2

2 tablespoons red wine
vinegar
1 tablespoon water
2 teaspoons minced onion
2 teaspoons soy sauce
1 clove garlic, minced
¼ teaspoon dried whole
rosemary, crushed
¼ teaspoon dried whole thyme,
crushed
Pepper to taste
2 (5-ounce) lamb chops, 1"
thick

Turn this delightful entrée into an elegant dish. Serve it with Bordelaise Sauce (Chapter 7) and garnish with fresh mint.

1. In a shallow 1-quart casserole dish, combine vinegar, water, onion, soy sauce, garlic, rosemary, thyme, and pepper. Add lamb chops to marinade and turn until well coated. Cover and refrigerate for at least 4 hours.

2. Drain lamb chops. Reserve marinade.

3. Preheat broiler or prepare grill.

4. Broil 5 inches from heating element (or pop on the grill) for about 5 minutes on each side, depending on your choice of doneness. Baste frequently with marinade.

5. Serve warm.

Skillet Lemony Lamb Chops

No muss, no fuss—a skillet meal that is quick and easy that tastes like you've been slaving over a hot stove for hours!

1. Preheat broiler. Place lamb chops on broiler rack under broiler. Broil until brown on both sides.

2. Place chops in a medium nonstick skillet.

3. In a small bowl, combine water, lemon zest, Worcestershire sauce, salt, oregano, rosemary, and freshly ground pepper. Whisk until well blended. Pour mixture over lamb chops in skillet.

4. Cover and cook over medium-low heat for about 30 minutes or until chops are tender.

Serves 2

2 (6-ounce) lamb chops, ¾" thick
3 tablespoons water
¼ teaspoon lemon zest
2 teaspoons Worcestershire sauce
¼ teaspoon salt
¼ teaspoon dried oregano
¼ teaspoon dried rosemary, crushed
Freshly ground pepper to taste

Grecian Grilled Skewers

Serves 2

½ pound lean boneless lamb
2 tablespoons white wine
  vinegar
2 tablespoons water
1 tablespoon dry sherry
2 teaspoons chopped fresh
  parsley
1 teaspoon sugar
¾ teaspoon dried whole
  rosemary, crushed
¼ teaspoon garlic salt
¼ teaspoon pepper
1 small green pepper
6 medium-sized fresh mushrooms
4 cherry tomatoes

These kebabs taste excellent grilled. Soak wooden kebab skewers in water to avoid any unwanted grill fires.

1. Cut lamb into 1" cubes.

2. In a small bowl, combine vinegar, water, sherry, parsley, sugar, rosemary, garlic salt, and pepper. Stir until well blended. Add cubed lamb. Stir until lamb is well coated. Cover and refrigerate overnight.

3. Seed green pepper and cut into 8 pieces. Place green pepper on a microwave-safe plate. Cover and microwave on high for 2 minutes.

4. Drain lamb. Discard marinade.

5. Alternate lamb and vegetables on four 10" wooden skewers. Place skewers on a microwave-safe roasting rack. Cover with waxed paper. Microwave on 50 percent power for 5–6 minutes.

6. Rearrange kebabs and microwave for another 5 minutes or until desired degree of doneness. Note: If you're a grill master, these are awesome prepared on the grill. Just watch them closely so they don't burn!

Score Points for Lamb!

When you're talking nutrition and red meat, lamb scores points in high nutritional values! An excellent source of protein and much easier to digest than other meats, lamb is also a rich source of iron, calcium, potassium, phosphorus, and B complex vitamins. Buy lean lamb so your kebabs don't turn out greasy.

Lamb with Fruit and Nut Sauce

This is a beautiful entrée to serve for special occasions. Serve it for a holiday entrée and you'll probably start a tradition!

1. In a small bowl, combine apricots, beef broth, currants, and brandy, stirring well. Cover and refrigerate for at least 8 hours.

2. Place lamb between two sheets of heavy-duty plastic wrap. Using a meat mallet, flatten to ½" thickness. Dredge in flour.

3. Coat a skillet with cooking spray. Add oil and place over medium-high heat until hot. Add lamb. Cook for 5 minutes on each side until lightly browned.

4. Add apricot mixture and pecans. Cover, reduce heat, and simmer until lamb is tender, about 15 minutes.

5. Place lamb on 4 individual plates and spoon apricot mixture over lamb. Serve immediately.

Serves 4

8 dried apricots, cut into strips
½ cup beef broth
¼ cup currants
¼ cup brandy
4 (4-ounce) slices lean bone-less leg of lamb
2 tablespoons flour
Nonstick cooking spray
2 teaspoons oil
1 tablespoon toasted chopped pecans

Seafood

chapter fourteen

Baked Salmon with Buttered Thyme Potatoes

Serves 2

2 baking potatoes, peeled
2 tablespoons margarine,
    softened, divided
Salt and fresh ground pepper
2 tablespoons minced shallots
4 sprigs fresh thyme
2 (6-ounce) salmon fillets

This dish certainly makes a very different and attractive presentation—it's almost as impressive as the flavor.

1. Preheat oven to 375°F. Slice potatoes into ¼" slices.

2. Using 1½ tablespoons of the margarine, coat the bottom of a large, heavy oven-proof skillet. Place half the potato slices so they overlap, covering a 5" × 5" area. Arrange the remaining potato slices in another cluster following the same overlapping arrangement.

3. Sprinkle with salt, freshly ground pepper, and shallots. Top each cluster with remaining margarine and a fresh thyme sprig. Place a salmon fillet on top of each potato cluster with skin side up. Place skillet over medium-high heat. Cook for 5 minutes without disturbing.

4. Transfer skillet to preheated oven. Bake for about 14 minutes, watching closely so potatoes don't scorch. Remove from oven when potatoes are golden and salmon is pale pink.

5. At serving time, use a metal spatula to flip each salmon cluster over so potatoes are on top. Garnish with remaining thyme sprigs. Serve warm.

Sesame Ginger Salmon

Grill this salmon dish instead of broiling it for an even richer flavor.

1. Combine sesame oil, brown sugar, teriyaki sauce, and ginger in a blender. Process until well blended.

2. Place salmon fillets in a plastic container. Pour half the marinade over them. Cover and refrigerate for 60 minutes. Reserve the other half of the marinade.

3. Remove salmon from refrigerator. Discard marinade.

4. Place fish in a shallow baking dish. Baste with reserved marinade.

5. Coat broiler pan with cooking spray. Place salmon on broiler pan. Broil for approximately 5 minutes per side until the outside is crispy and the inside is pale pink.

Salmon: Pretty in Pink

There are endless ways to prepare the lovely pink-hued salmon, which is an all-time favorite among fresh fish lovers. Even folks who don't care for fish are open to ordering fresh salmon when it's on the menu! Eating this incredibly nutritious pinkish fish helps keep your health in the pink as well!

Serves 4

½ cup sesame oil
3 tablespoons light brown sugar
¼ cup teriyaki sauce
1½ teaspoons grated fresh ginger
2 (8-ounce) salmon fillets
Nonstick cooking spray

Poached Salmon

Serves 8

2 cups water
1 cup dry white wine
1 lemon, sliced
1 small onion, sliced, optional
2 bay leaves
8 black peppercorns
4 dill sprigs
1 teaspoon Tabasco sauce
¼ teaspoon salt
4 (8-ounce) salmon steaks

Poaching is an extremely delicate way to prepare salmon. Because of the gentle cooking, the flavor of the fish will shine through, so make sure that you're buying high-quality salmon from a reputable store, and using it on the same day you purchase it.

1. In a large skillet combine water, wine, lemon, onion, bay leaves, peppercorn, dill, Tabasco, and salt. Bring to a boil.

2. Reduce heat. Cover and simmer for 15 minutes.

3. Add salmon to skillet. Simmer covered until fish flakes easily when fork tested, about 15 minutes.

4. Serve warm or chilled.

Grilled Salmon with Creamy Tarragon Sauce

Substitute fresh herbs for dried whenever possible. The fresh herbs add more flavor and punch than dried herbs ever could.

1. In a small glass bowl combine yogurt, mayonnaise, green onions, tarragon, lime juice, and hot pepper sauce. Cover and refrigerate for at least 1½ hours.

2. Remove skin from salmon. Cut into four equal portions. Brush with olive oil.

3. Grill salmon over medium heat until fish flakes easily with fork, about 5 minutes on each side. If you prefer, broil salmon for about 4 minutes on each side, 5 inches from broiler.

4. Serve with fresh tarragon sauce.

Serves 4

1 cup plain soy yogurt
1 tablespoon mayonnaise
¼ cup minced green onions
1 tablespoon minced fresh
  tarragon
2 teaspoons lime juice
1 teaspoon hot pepper sauce
16-ounce salmon fillet, 1"
  thick, skinned
1 tablespoon olive oil

Snapper with Lemon Dill Spinach

Serves 6

Nonstick cooking spray
6 (4-ounce) skinless snapper fillets
1 tablespoon fresh lemon juice
4 teaspoons Dijon mustard
½ cup finely chopped fresh dill
1 teaspoon extra-virgin olive oil
2 (10-ounce) bags fresh spinach leaves, stems removed, washed and drained
1 garlic clove, minced
1 lemon, quartered lengthwise

Feel free to substitute the snapper with another type of similar fish in this recipe if snapper isn't your cup of tea or isn't readily available.

1. Preheat oven to 400°F. Spray a glass baking dish with cooking spray.

2. Arrange snapper fillets in dish. Sprinkle with lemon juice. Spread Dijon mustard over each fillet.

3. Reserve 1 tablespoon of the fresh dill. Sprinkle remaining dill over snapper fillets. Bake until just cooked through, 18–20 minutes.

4. While fish is baking, heat olive oil in a large skillet over medium heat. Add spinach and minced garlic. Stir together for about 4 minutes or until spinach is wilted.

5. Using tongs, divide spinach on plates without pan juices. Place hot fish fillets over spinach. Sprinkle remaining fresh dill on top. Garnish with lemon wedges. Serve immediately.

Snapper Surprises

There are seventeen different varieties of "snapper." The two most popular varieties are yellowtail snapper and red snapper. On the healthy side, snapper is low in calories and contains almost no saturated fat. It packs plenty of protein, calcium, and iron, too!

Baked Halibut with Artichoke Hearts

Serve this fish entrée with a fresh garden salad.

1. Preheat oven to 375°F.

2. Coat a medium skillet with cooking spray and heat skillet over medium heat. Add onion and parsley. Sauté until tender.

3. Drain and chop artichoke hearts. Stir in artichoke hearts, mayonnaise, fresh lemon juice, garlic powder, and red pepper. Set aside.

4. Rinse halibut with cold water and pat dry. Place halibut steaks in a large aluminum foil–lined shallow roasting pan. Spoon artichoke mixture evenly over steaks.

5. Bake, uncovered, until steaks flake easily when fork tested, about 10 minutes. Serve on warmed plates.

Serves 8

Nonstick cooking spray
¼ cup chopped green onion
2 tablespoons chopped fresh parsley
1 (14-ounce) can artichoke hearts
3 tablespoons mayonnaise
1 tablespoon fresh lemon juice
½ teaspoon garlic powder
¼ teaspoon red pepper flakes
8 (4-ounce) halibut steaks

Oven-Fried Trout

Serves 4

4 (4-ounce) trout fillets
1 tablespoon olive oil
¼ teaspoon salt
¼ teaspoon garlic powder
¼ teaspoon pepper
⅓ cup cornflake crumbs
Nonstick cooking spray
Lemon slices
Fresh parsley sprigs

The distinctive flavor of trout really comes through in the oven-fried method used in this recipe.

1. Preheat oven to 500°F. Rinse trout with cold water and pat dry.

2. Brush fillets with oil. Sprinkle with salt, garlic powder, and pepper. Dredge in cornflake crumbs.

3. Coat a 12" × 8" × 2" baking dish with cooking spray. Arrange fillets in a single layer in baking dish.

4. Bake, uncovered, until fillets flake easily when tested with a fork, about 10 minutes.

5. Carefully transfer to a warmed serving platter. Garnish with lemon slices and parsley. Serve immediately.

Sole and Veggies En Papillote

A meal all wrapped up in a little packet makes for easy and mess-free cooking and easy serving.

1. Place margarine in a 1-quart casserole dish. Microwave on high until melted, about 20 seconds.

2. Add red pepper, carrots, broccoli, and garlic to casserole. Stir to combine ingredients. Cover and microwave on high until just crisp-tender, 2–3 minutes. Set aside.

3. Cut four 16" × 12" pieces of parchment paper. Then cut each into a large heart shape. Fold heart in half and then open flat.

4. Place a fillet along center fold on each sheet of paper. Sprinkle fillets with lemon juice, paprika, and pepper. Top each fillet with equal amounts of vegetable mixture. Fold paper edges over to seal securely.

5. Place two pouches on a microwave-safe 12" platter. Microwave at high for 3–4 minutes; set aside and keep warm. Repeat process and serve.

En Papillote

Cooking en papillote is fun and fancy. You can wrap up just about any ingredients that you like in parchment paper and cook them en papillote! It delivers crispy, crunchy veggies with freshness extraordinaire and seals in the natural juices of fish and meats.

Serves 12–16

1 tablespoon margarine
1 sweet red pepper, seeded and sliced
2 medium carrots, cut into julienne strips
⅔ cup fresh broccoli florets
1 clove garlic, crushed
4 (1-pound) sole fillets
2 teaspoons fresh lemon juice
¼ teaspoon paprika
½ teaspoon pepper

Blackened Bass

1 pound bass fillets, ½" thick
2 tablespoons water
1 tablespoon hot sauce
2 teaspoons onion powder
2 teaspoons garlic powder
2 tablespoons paprika
1 teaspoon dried whole thyme,
    crushed
1 teaspoon dried whole
    oregano, crushed
2 teaspoons pepper
1 teaspoon red pepper
Nonstick cooking spray
1 tablespoon margarine

Bass is great eating (and fun to fish for, too)! If you like your fish blackened a bit, this recipe will suit your fancy!

1. Rinse fillets under cold water and leave damp. Place in a shallow dish.

2. Combine 2 tablespoons water and hot sauce in a small bowl. Spoon mixture over fillets. Cover and marinate in refrigerator for at least 2 hours, turning once.

3. Remove fillets from marinade. Discard marinade. In a small flat dish, combine onion powder, garlic powder, paprika, thyme, oregano, pepper, and red pepper. Dredge fillets in spices and coat well.

4. Coat a large cast-iron skillet with cooking spray. Add margarine. Place over medium-high heat until margarine melts. Add fillets. Cook for 2–3 minutes on each side, turning carefully. If you prefer, cook the fillets on a grill. Keep in mind that you're cooking "blackened bass" and it will have a charred look.

Baked Sea Bass and Veggies

A complete meal all under one roof—well, under the lid of one skillet, anyway!

1. Coat a large skillet with cooking spray. Melt margarine in skillet over medium heat.

2. Add potato, onion, carrot, and garlic. Cover and cook for 3 minutes. Add red pepper, chopped tomato, chicken broth, ripe olives, capers, and thyme. Cover and cook until veggies are crisp-tender, about 15 minutes.

3. Place fillets over vegetable mixture in skillet. Cover and cook until fish flakes easily when fork tested, about 10 minutes.

4. Using a slotted spoon, transfer fillets and veggie mixture to a warmed serving platter.

5. Drizzle lemon juice evenly over dish and serve immediately.

Serves 6

Nonstick cooking spray
2 tablespoons margarine
2 cups finely chopped red
  potato
1 cup chopped onion
¾ cup chopped carrot
2 teaspoons minced garlic
2 cups thinly sliced sweet red
  pepper
2 cups peeled, seeded, and
  chopped tomato
1 cup chicken broth
3 tablespoons sliced ripe
  olives
2 teaspoons capers, drained
½ teaspoon dried whole thyme
6 (4-ounce) sea bass fillets,
  1" thick
2 tablespoons fresh lemon
  juice

Orange Marinated Swordfish

Serves 4

¼ cup unsweetened orange juice
3 tablespoons minced fresh mint
1 tablespoon peeled, grated gingerroot
1 tablespoon grated orange rind
2 tablespoons bourbon (optional)
2 (8-ounce) swordfish steaks, ¾" thick
4 orange slices, ¼" thick
Nonstick cooking spray
Fresh mint sprigs (optional)

Swordfish is a distinctively flavored fish on its own. Adding this marinade of mingled flavors makes for an entrée that will make your mouth sing!

1. Combine orange juice, fresh mint, grated gingerroot, orange rind, and bourbon (if desired) in a large, shallow dish.

2. Place swordfish steaks and orange slices in a single layer in the dish. Turn to coat evenly. Cover and place in refrigerator for at least 30 minutes. Turn once while swordfish is marinating.

3. Coat grill rack with cooking spray. Place swordfish steaks on medium-hot grill. Cover and cook until fish flakes easily when fork tested, about 5 minutes on each side.

4. Transfer steaks to a warm serving platter. Cut each steak in half.

5. Place orange slices on grill rack. Cover and cook for 2 minutes on each side. Cut each orange slice into thirds. Arrange with fish on serving platter. Garnish with fresh mint sprigs, if desired.

Swordfish Trivia

Swordfish have long, round bodies. They have no teeth and no scales. They grow to a maximum size of 14 feet. Swordfish are rich in vitamin B_{12} and a good source of omega-3 fatty acids.

Flaky Fish Tacos

Any firm-flesh white fish in fillet form can be used for this recipe. Haddock, cod, and whiting are usually easy to find, and all taste delicious in this recipe.

1. In a large, heavy saucepan, combine chicken broth, lime juice, jalapeño juice, and salt. Bring to a boil.

2. Add the fish fillets and return to simmering point. Reduce heat, cover, and simmer until fish becomes opaque, about 7 minutes. Be careful not to overcook fish. Drain well.

3. Place fish in a bowl. Remove any skin or bones. Flake fish with a fork.

4. Warm taco shells. Put a layer of lettuce in each taco shell. Spoon the flaked fish on top. Add a layer of green onions and a layer of diced tomatoes.

5. Top with salsa, if desired. Serve at once.

Serves 6

3 cups chicken broth
1 teaspoon fresh lime juice
1 tablespoon juice from a jar of
   pickled jalapeños
¼ teaspoon salt
1 pound fillet of any firm-
   fleshed white fish
12 warmed taco shells
2 cups shredded lettuce
3 green onions, including
   green part, thinly sliced
1 medium-sized tomato, diced
Salsa (optional)

Catfish Gumbo

Serves 8

1 cup celery, chopped
1 cup onion, chopped
1 cup green pepper, chopped
2 cloves garlic, minced
3 tablespoons olive oil
4 cups beef broth
1 (16-ounce) can whole tomatoes, cut up
1 bay leaf
1 teaspoon salt
½ teaspoon dried thyme
½ teaspoon ground red pepper
½ teaspoon dried oregano, crushed
2 pounds catfish fillets, cut into bite-sized pieces
1 (10-ounce) package frozen sliced okra
4 cups hot cooked rice

Gumbo warms the cockles of your heart and your entire body! You can use this gumbo recipe as a base recipe and substitute whatever type of fish appeals to you.

1. In a large, heavy kettle, cook celery, onion, green pepper, and garlic in hot oil until tender.

2. Stir in beef broth, tomatoes, bay leaf, salt, thyme, red pepper, and oregano. Bring to a boil. Reduce heat and simmer, covered, for 15 minutes.

3. Add catfish and okra. Return to boiling.

4. Reduce heat, cover, and simmer until fish flakes easily, about 15 minutes.

5. Serve in soup bowls over hot cooked rice.

Scallop Ceviche

If this is your first time making ceviche you'll find it interesting that the lime juice brings about a chemical change similar to that produced by heat. The scallops will become opaque.

1. Place scallops in a shallow dish. Add enough lime juice to cover. Turn scallops to coat all sides.

2. Cover dish with plastic wrap and refrigerate for at least 4 hours. Scallops will become opaque. Drain scallops and discard juice.

3. In a medium bowl combine marinated scallops, chilies, tomatoes, onion, chopped dill, and olive oil. Salt to taste. Cover and refrigerate until ready to serve.

4. At serving time, peel and slice avocado. Brush avocado with lime juice to prevent it from discoloring.

5. Garnish scallop ceviche with avocado and fresh dill. Serve with crackers.

Ceviche Trivia

Ceviche isn't considered safe to eat unless the fish has been frozen to 31°F for 15 hours or unless you use sushi-grade scallops. The acid doesn't cook the fish; it just denatures the protein. Seviche is a Mediterranean method of preserving raw fish. The Latin American Spanish word *seviche* comes from the Iberian Spanish escabeche, also called chebbeci in Sicily, a word that means "marinated fish."

Serves 6

1½ pounds scallops
Juice of 6 limes or lemons
2 green chilies, seeded and finely sliced
3 large tomatoes, skinned, deseeded and diced
1 small red onion, finely chopped
6 tablespoons chopped dill
⅓ cup olive oil
Salt, to taste
1 avocado and a few sprigs of dill to garnish

Oregano Scallop Medley

Serves 4

1 pound fresh bay scallops
Nonstick cooking spray
2 teaspoons olive oil
1 cup sliced fresh mushrooms
2 green onions with tops, sliced
1 tablespoon dried whole oregano
12 cherry tomatoes, cut in half

Most seafood is versatile, and scallops are no exception. Couple the rich taste of scallops with oregano and you have a very different approach to serving bay scallops!

1. Rinse scallops with cold water and pat dry.

2. Coat a large skillet with cooking spray; add olive oil and place over medium heat until hot. Add scallops. Sauté for 3 minutes.

3. Remove scallops from skillet, discarding liquid. Add mushrooms, green onions, and oregano to skillet. Sauté together for 3 minutes.

4. Add reserved scallops and tomatoes to skillet. Sauté until thoroughly heated, about 1 minute.

5. Serve immediately.

Scallops in Tangerine Sauce

If you're serving these scallops in tangerine sauce to guests, you might as well print out some recipe cards before they arrive!

1. In a small saucepan, combine clam juice, fresh parsley, lemon juice, thyme, basil, and pepper. Bring to a boil. Reduce heat and simmer for 10 minutes. Add scallops and cook until scallops are opaque, about 6 minutes.

2. Drain scallops and reserve ½ cup liquid. Set scallops aside, cover, and keep warm. Cook fettuccine according to package directions. Drain well and set aside, keeping warm.

3. In a small, heavy saucepan, combine reserved ½ cup liquid, tangerine juice, and 1 tablespoon lemon juice. Bring mixture to a boil over medium heat.

4. Combine cornstarch and water in a small screw-top jar and shake until lumps are gone. Slowly add to juice mixture. Reduce heat and cook until mixture begins to bubble and is thickened, stirring constantly.

5. Transfer fettuccine to a warm serving platter. Place scallops on top and spoon tangerine sauce over scallops.

Serves 4

1 cup clam juice
2 tablespoons chopped fresh parsley
1 tablespoon lemon juice
1 teaspoon dried whole thyme
1 teaspoon dried whole basil
¼ teaspoon pepper
1 pound fresh bay scallops
4 ounces spinach fettuccine, uncooked
⅔ cup fresh squeezed tangerine juice
1 tablespoon lemon juice
1 tablespoon cornstarch
¼ cup water

Garlic Shrimp

Serves 6

6 cups water
2 pounds unpeeled large fresh
  shrimp
Nonstick cooking spray
¼ cup green onions
2 teaspoons minced garlic
¼ cup dry white wine
¼ cup water
1 teaspoon lemon juice
½ teaspoon salt
½ teaspoon coarsely ground
  black pepper
1 teaspoon dried whole dill
  weed
1 teaspoon chopped fresh
  parsley
3 cups hot cooked rice
  (optional)

A large helping of garlic can be good when preparing a shrimp dish like this. Use as much or as little garlic as you desire.

1. In a large stockpot, bring 6 cups water to a boil. Add shrimp and return to a boil. Reduce heat and simmer for about 4 minutes.

2. Drain shrimp well and rinse with cold water. Peel and de-vein shrimp.

3. Coat a large skillet with cooking spray and heat over medium heat. Add green onions and garlic to skillet. Sauté until green onions are tender.

4. Add shrimp, white wine, water, lemon juice, salt, and pepper. Cook over medium heat for about 5 minutes or until shrimp turns light pink, stirring occasionally. Note: Be careful not to overcook shrimp as it will be rubbery. Stir in dill weed and parsley.

5. Serve over rice, if desired.

Mandarin Shrimp and Veggie Stir-Fry

Orange marmalade combined with fresh ginger and garlic with shrimp as the base of the recipe is bound to be a pleaser. This is a great dish on its own, but add rice to complement it.

1. Peel and de-vein shrimp. In a small bowl, combine orange marmalade, soy sauce, vinegar, Tabasco, and cornstarch. Stir well to dissolve cornstarch. Set aside.

2. Place a large skillet or wok over high heat. Heat skillet for 1 minute and add olive oil. Heat oil for 30 seconds. Add ginger, garlic, and shrimp. Stir-fry shrimp until they begin to turn pink, about 3 minutes. Remove shrimp from skillet and set aside.

3. Add the peppers and broccoli to skillet. Cook on high heat for 1 minute. Reduce heat to medium. Add water and cover. Cook veggies until tender, about 5 minutes.

4. Remove cover. Return heat to high. Add shrimp and marmalade mixture. Cook shrimp for another 2 minutes until sauce is thickened and shrimp are completely cooked.

5. Stir in green onions. Serve with cooked rice if desired.

Shrimp Tips

When you're buying fresh shrimp, make sure the meat is firm. If you're buying frozen shrimp, purchase shrimp in a clear plastic bag so you can see any freezer burn. You can grill 'em, and they're great sautéed, roasted, stir-fried, baked, or in a shrimp cocktail. Shrimp are rich in vitamin B12, niacin, omega-3 fatty acids, iron, zinc, and copper.

Serves 6

24 fresh jumbo shrimp
1 cup orange marmalade
3 tablespoons soy sauce
2 tablespoons white vinegar
2 teaspoons Tabasco sauce
1½ tablespoons cornstarch
2 tablespoons light olive oil
1 tablespoon chopped fresh
    ginger
1 tablespoon chopped fresh
    garlic
1 red bell pepper, chopped
1 green bell pepper, chopped
3 cups broccoli florets
½ cup water
1 cup chopped green onions

Rice and Pasta

chapter fifteen

Pistachio Basmati Rice

Serves 6

10 ounces basmati rice
2 bunches green onions
2 tablespoons olive oil
1 cup pistachio nuts, shelled,
  coarsely chopped
1 teaspoon crushed red pepper flakes

Pistachio nuts add a wonderful flavor and crunch to already delightful basmati rice. This full-flavored dish is also full of vitamins, protein, and essential nutrients.

1. Cook rice in a large, covered pan according to package directions.

2. Rinse green onions and cut into ½" diagonal slices.

3. Heat 1 tablespoon of the olive oil in a small skillet. Add green onions and sauté over medium heat for a short minute.

4. Stir in pistachio nuts and cook for another minute, stirring constantly. Set aside.

5. At serving time, uncover rice and fold in red pepper flakes, green onions, and nuts with a fork. Drizzle remaining oil over rice. Serve immediately.

Basmati Rice Ramblings

Did you know that basmati rice has a delicate reputation? It is known for being the most aromatic, delicate, and delicious member of the rice family! To prepare the rice, rinse it several times in cold water and let it soak for about 30 minutes. This will help give the rice its characteristic fluffiness.

Wild Rice with Cranberries and Toasted Pine Nuts

Talk about tasty! The pine nuts lend a little crunch, and the dried cranberries add just the right touch of sweetness.

1. Remove stems from green onions and rinse. Slice green onions into ¼" diagonal pieces.

2. Heat 1 tablespoon of the olive oil in a small skillet.

3. Add green onions and sauté over medium-high heat for about 2 minutes, stirring constantly. Set skillet aside.

4. Prepare wild rice according to package instructions.

5. After rice has cooked, fold in green onions, dried cranberries, toasted pine nuts, and the remaining tablespoon of olive oil. Heat for 1 minute. Serve warm.

Serves 4

2 bunches green onions
2 tablespoons olive oil
1 (5-ounce) package wild rice
2 ounces dried cranberries
1¾ ounces toasted pine nuts

Orange Rice

Serves 6

2 cups water
2 tablespoons grated orange peel
½ cup orange juice
½ teaspoon salt
1 cup uncooked, long-grain rice
½ cup raisins
Orange slice for garnish (optional)

Because of the citrus combo with the long-grain rice, this is a perfect complement to chicken and fish.

1. In a medium saucepan, combine water, orange peel, orange juice, and salt. Bring to a boil.

2. Stir in rice and raisins. Return to boiling.

3. Reduce heat and cook, covered, over low heat until rice is tender and liquid is absorbed, about 25 minutes. Serve hot with orange slice garnish, if desired.

Baked Wild Rice with Herbs

This fine potpourri of a recipe fills the house with warm, inviting aromas while it's cooking.

1. Preheat oven to 350°F.

2. Rinse the wild rice carefully. Let soak according to package directions if called for.

3. Melt margarine in a large skillet over medium heat. Add celery, onion, and mushrooms, cooking while stirring constantly until vegetables are translucent.

4. Drain wild rice. Add rice to skillet. Cook, stirring constantly for 2 minutes. Place wild rice mixture in a 2-quart baking dish. Stir in 4 cups of the chicken broth. Add herbs and seasonings and stir to combine.

5. Cover and bake for 1½ hours. Stir a couple of times during baking. If rice mixture becomes dry, add more broth during the last 20 minutes.

The Caviar of All Grains

Wild rice is referred to as the caviar of all grains. With its nutty textured seed and sweet taste it is definitely the rice of choice for creating very special dishes. It is truly one of the most versatile and flavorful grains.

Serves 8

1 cup uncooked wild rice
¼ cup margarine
1 cup chopped celery
1 cup chopped onion
½ cup sliced mushrooms
4½ cups chicken broth
1 tablespoon chopped fresh parsley
¼ teaspoon thyme
¼ teaspoon dried basil
½ teaspoon salt
½ teaspoon black pepper

Curried Rice

Serves 2

⅔ cup water, divided
2 tablespoons chopped green onion
⅓ cup parboiled rice, uncooked
½ teaspoon chicken-flavored bouillon granules
¼ teaspoon curry powder
Dash of pepper
Green onion fans (optional)

Eat curried rice on its own or add a bit of chicken or pork to bolster the flavor.

1. Combine ⅓ cup water and onion in a 1-quart casserole dish.

2. Cover and microwave on high for 1 minute.

3. Add another ⅓ cup water, rice, bouillon granules, curry powder, and pepper to casserole. Stir well.

4. Cover and microwave on high until water boils, about 3 minutes. Stir well.

5. Cover and microwave at 50 percent power until liquid is absorbed, about 10 minutes. Let stand for 4 minutes before serving. Garnish with green onion fans if desired.

Spanish Rice with Beef

Skillet meals are becoming more and more popular for good reason. They come together rather quickly, and it's all in one pan!

1. In a large, heavy skillet, cook ground beef, onion, and green pepper until meat is browned.

2. Drain in a colander and pat dry with a paper towel. Wipe pan drippings from skillet with a paper towel.

3. Return meat mixture to skillet.

4. Stir in tomatoes, water, rice, chili powder, oregano, salt, red pepper, and garlic powder. Bring to a boil.

5. Reduce heat, cover and simmer until rice is tender, stirring occasionally, about 30 minutes.

Serves 6

1 pound lean ground beef
1 medium onion, chopped
1 medium-sized green pepper, chopped
2 (16-ounce) cans stewed tomatoes, undrained
1 cup water
1 cup uncooked rice
1½ teaspoons chili powder
¾ teaspoon dried whole oregano
½ teaspoon salt
¼ teaspoon red pepper
½ teaspoon garlic powder

Fiesta Rice

Serves 4

Nonstick cooking spray
1 teaspoon light olive oil
½ cup chopped sweet red
    pepper
¼ cup chopped onion
1 clove garlic, minced
1¼ cups chicken broth
½ cup long-grain rice, un-
    cooked
½ cup frozen whole-kernel
    corn, thawed
½ cup salsa
½ cup drained canned black
    beans
1 tablespoon chopped fresh
    cilantro
¼ teaspoon salt
Orange slices (optional)
Fresh cilantro sprigs (optional)

This intensely-flavored rice comes together in a flash using frozen and pantry items. Some people find that their palates are sensitive to cilantro, so consider serving it on the side, instead of mixed into the rice.

1. Coat a large saucepan with cooking spray.

2. Heat olive oil over medium-high heat. Add red pepper, onion, and garlic. Sauté until crisp-tender.

3. Add broth, rice, corn, and salsa. Bring to a boil.

4. Reduce heat, cover, and simmer for 20 minutes. Remove from heat. Let stand until liquid is absorbed, about 5 minutes.

5. Stir in beans, chopped cilantro, and salt. Garnish with orange slices and cilantro sprigs, if desired.

Seafood Risotto

Risotto is an elegant dish, perfect for entertaining. Do all your prep work ahead of time and store ingredients in the fridge, and the dish will only take about 30 minutes of cooking time.

1. In a medium saucepan, combine water and broth and heat over low heat. Keep mixture on heat.

2. In a large saucepan, heat olive oil over medium heat. Add onion and garlic; cook and stir until crisp-tender, about 3 minutes. Add rice; cook and stir for 3 minutes.

3. Start adding broth mixture, a cup at a time, stirring frequently, adding liquid when previous addition is absorbed. When only 1 cup of broth remains to be added, stir in celery, dill, wine, fish fillets, shrimp, and scallops to rice mixture. Add last cup of broth.

4. Cook, stirring constantly, for 5–7 minutes or until fish is cooked and rice is tender and creamy. Stir in butter and serve.

Serves 6

2 cups water
2½ cups low-sodium chicken broth
2 tablespoons olive oil
1 onion, minced
3 cloves garlic, minced
1½ cups Arborio rice
1 cup chopped celery
1 tablespoon fresh dill weed
¼ cup dry white wine
½ pound sole fillets
¼ pound small raw shrimp
½ pound bay scallops
1 tablespoon butter

Herbed Rice Sauté

Serves 6

Nonstick cooking spray
1 tablespoon margarine
1 cup uncooked rice
1 cup chopped onion
2¼ cups water
1 teaspoon dried whole
    rosemary
½ teaspoon dried whole
    marjoram
½ teaspoon dried whole
    savory
2 chicken-flavored bouillon
    cubes

A little tip about rosemary: If it's possible to use fresh rosemary any time a recipe calls for rosemary, use it!

1. Coat a large, heavy skillet with cooking spray.

2. Add margarine and place over medium-high heat until margarine is melted. Add rice and onion, sautéing until rice is lightly browned.

3. Add water, rosemary, marjoram, whole savory, and bouillon cubes. Stir to dissolve bouillon. Bring to a boil.

4. Reduce heat and simmer, covered, until water is absorbed and rice is tender, about 25 minutes.

Brown Rice Pilaf

Brown rice is so good for you. In this recipe, brown rice soaks up these added flavors to please your palate.

1. Preheat oven to 350°F.

2. Combine broth, brown rice, onion, mushrooms, pepper, and thyme in a 1-quart casserole dish.

3. Cover and bake rice mixture for 1 hour.

4. Add celery to rice mixture. Cover again and bake until liquid is absorbed and celery is tender, about 15 minutes.

Serves 4

1¼ cups chicken broth
½ cup uncooked brown rice
½ cup chopped onion
1 (3-ounce) jar sliced mushrooms, drained
¼ teaspoon pepper
½ teaspoon dried whole thyme
½ cup thinly sliced celery

Italian Rice

Serves 8

1 (9-ounce) package frozen artichoke hearts, thawed
1½ cups water
¾ cup long-grain rice, un-cooked
1 tablespoon olive oil
⅔ cup sweet red pepper strips
½ cup frozen baby peas, thawed
½ cup sliced green onions
1 clove garlic, minced
3 tablespoons bottled Italian dressing
1 teaspoon dried Italian seasoning

Quick, easy, and full of flavor! Artichoke hearts take center stage in this very different combination rice recipe. And this dish is full of color, too!

1. Coarsely chop thawed artichoke hearts. Set aside.

2. Bring 1½ cups water to a boil in a medium saucepan. Stir in long-grain rice. Reduce heat and cover. Simmer rice until all liquid is absorbed and rice is tender, about 20 minutes.

3. In a large skillet, heat olive oil over medium heat. Add chopped artichoke hearts, red pepper strips, baby peas, green onions, and minced garlic. Sauté until veggies are crisp-tender, about 5 minutes.

4. Combine rice, sautéed vegetables, Italian dressing, and Italian seasoning.

5. Toss gently until evenly coated.

Mexican Rice

You be the judge of the green chilies; you don't have to use the whole can. Decide for yourself how much or how little spice you want.

1. Preheat oven to 350°F.

2. Coat a 2-quart casserole dish with cooking spray.

3. Combine long-grain rice, sun-dried tomatoes, sweet red pepper, green onions, green chilies, cumin seeds, and garlic in casserole dish.

4. Bring beef broth to a boil in a medium saucepan. Pour broth over rice mixture.

5. Cover and bake until liquid is absorbed and rice is tender, about 40 minutes.

Serves 8

Nonstick cooking spray
1 cup long-grain rice, uncooked
¾ cup chopped dry sun-dried
  tomatoes
½ cup chopped sweet red
  pepper
¼ cup chopped green onions
1 (4½-ounce) can chopped
  green chilies
2 teaspoons cumin seeds
1 clove garlic, minced
2½ cups beef broth

Oriental Wild Rice

Serves 6

2½ cups water
1 cup wild rice, uncooked
1 small sweet red pepper
4 green onions
Nonstick cooking spray
1 tablespoon dark sesame oil
2 cups broccoli florets
1 cup fresh bean sprouts
⅔ cup diagonally sliced carrot
1 tablespoon sesame seeds
1 teaspoon peeled, minced
   gingerroot
2 teaspoons soy sauce

This is good leftover the next day. Pop it in your lunch for an added treat.

1. Combine water and rice in a medium saucepan. Bring to a boil. Reduce heat, cover, and simmer until rice is tender, about 40 minutes. Drain and set aside.

2. Seed and cut red pepper into 1" pieces; cut onions into 1" pieces.

3. Coat a large skillet or wok with cooking spray. Drizzle sesame oil around top of wok or skillet, coating sides. Heat over medium-high heat.

4. Add red pepper, onions, broccoli, bean sprouts, carrots, sesame seeds, minced gingerroot, and soy sauce. Stir-fry all together for 3 minutes.

5. Cover and allow vegetables to steam until crisp-tender, about 6 minutes. Add rice. Stir-fry until mixture is thoroughly heated. Serve immediately.

Minted Couscous

When this couscous hits your mouth you'll probably think that those green peas are delivering that minty flavor. Mint is one of those herbs that can be described as both warm and cool; in this rice dish it's very cool!

1. Combine water, fresh mint, bouillon granules, and salt in a medium saucepan. Bring to a boil.

2. Remove from heat. Add couscous and peas.

3. Cover and let stand until liquid is absorbed and couscous is tender, about 5 minutes.

4. Fluff couscous with a fork.

5. Transfer from saucepan to a serving bowl. Garnish with fresh mint sprigs, if desired.

Serves 6

1¾ cups water
2 teaspoons minced fresh mint
1 teaspoon chicken-flavored
   bouillon granules
½ teaspoon salt
1 cup couscous, uncooked
¾ cup frozen peas, thawed
Fresh mint sprigs (optional)

Harvest Couscous

Serves 6

2 cups water
¾ cup peeled, diced sweet potato
¼ cup diced dried figs
⅓ cup diced dried apricots
½ teaspoon pumpkin pie spice
¾ cup couscous, uncooked

This dish has all the trappings of a favorite holiday dish.

1. Combine water, sweet potato, figs, apricots, and pumpkin pie spice in a medium saucepan. Bring to a boil.

2. Reduce heat, cover, and simmer until potato is tender, about 15 minutes.

3. Remove from heat. Add couscous.

4. Cover and let stand until liquid is absorbed and couscous is tender, about 5 minutes.

5. Fluff couscous with a fork. Transfer to a serving bowl.

Pasta with Broccoli Tomato Sauce

This recipe delivers a Mediterranean flavor to pasta. Bon appetit!

1. Steam broccoli over boiling water until crisp-tender, about 3 minutes. Remove from heat. Rinse with cold water.

2. Immerse tomatoes in boiling water for 12 seconds to blanch them. Slip skins off tomatoes. Set aside. Coarsely chop tomatoes.

3. Coat a large skillet with cooking spray. Heat olive oil over medium-high heat. Add tomatoes, garlic, red pepper flakes, Greek olives, parsley, salt, and pepper. Sauté for about 3 minutes. Add broccoli. Sauté for another 2 minutes.

4. Prepare pasta according to package instructions. Drain pasta and place on serving plate.

5. Ladle sauce over pasta, and serve.

Under Cover Tomatoes

If you purchase tomatoes that aren't as ripe as you'd like, pop them in a paper bag and put them on the countertop for one or two days. This will speed the ripening process.

Serves 4

2 cups fresh broccoli florets
2 large ripe tomatoes
Nonstick cooking spray
1 tablespoon olive oil
2 garlic cloves, minced
½ teaspoon red pepper flakes
10 Greek olives, sliced
½ cup coarsely chopped
 parsley
Salt and pepper to taste
½ pound angel hair pasta

Chicken Spaghetti

Serves 4

Nonstick cooking spray
2 teaspoons margarine
½ cup onion, minced
1 clove garlic, minced
4 boneless, skinless chicken
    breasts
1 (15-ounce) can tomatoes,
    puréed
1 (8-ounce) can tomato sauce
1 teaspoon basil
¼ teaspoon thyme
¼ teaspoon Italian seasoning
½ teaspoon salt
½ teaspoon pepper
4 cups cooked spaghetti

Chicken just soaks up the wonderful seasonings in this dish. Serve with a fresh garden salad and your meal is complete!

1. Coat a large skillet with cooking spray. Melt margarine over medium heat. Add onion and garlic. Sauté until lightly browned.

2. Cut each chicken breast into 8 pieces. Brown breasts with onion and garlic.

3. Add tomatoes and tomato sauce. Bring to a boil.

4. Reduce heat and add basil, thyme, Italian seasoning, salt, and pepper. Cover and simmer until chicken is tender, about 25 minutes.

5. Serve over hot cooked spaghetti.

Garden Pasta

Bring the garden to your table every time you get a chance, even in pasta dishes!

1. In a heavy medium saucepan, add tomatoes, celery, carrots, and onion. Cover tightly. Cook over medium heat for about 10 minutes, stirring occasionally and adjusting heat if too high.

2. Add sugar, basil, garlic powder, salt, pepper, and oregano. Cover and continue cooking over medium-low heat for an additional 5 minutes.

3. Add olive oil. Simmer until carrots are tender, about 30 minutes.

4. Cook spaghetti according to package directions. Drain.

5. Toss with sauce. Serve immediately.

Recipe Variation

Cut one or more of your favorite vegetables like broccoli, asparagus, or mushrooms into bite-sized pieces. Sauté veggies with minced garlic in lots of olive oil over high heat until crisp-tender. Serve over cooked pasta with the oil.

Serves 8

5 medium tomatoes, chopped
2 stalks celery, chopped
2 medium carrots, chopped
1 medium onion, chopped
1 teaspoon sugar
1 teaspoon basil
¼ teaspoon garlic powder
½ teaspoon salt
½ teaspoon pepper
½ teaspoon oregano
1 tablespoon olive oil
1 pound uncooked spaghetti

Spaghetti with Shrimp Sauce

Serves 4

Nonstick cooking spray
1 medium onion, chopped
1 medium-sized green pepper,
  chopped
½ cup chopped green onions
¼ cup chopped celery
4 cloves garlic, minced
1 (8-ounce) can tomato sauce
½ (10-ounce) can tomatoes
  with green chilies, undrained
  and chopped
¼ teaspoon salt
¼ teaspoon pepper
¼ teaspoon dried whole
  oregano
½ teaspoon dried whole
  rosemary
½ teaspoon dried whole thyme
¼ cup water
1 pound unpeeled fresh
  shrimp
4 ounces uncooked spaghetti

There's something incredibly palate-pleasing about the combination of seafood with pasta. Shrimp lovers will love this recipe!

1. Coat a large skillet with cooking spray. Heat over medium-high heat.

2. Add onion, green pepper, green onions, celery, and garlic. Sauté until vegetables are tender.

3. Add tomato sauce, tomatoes, seasonings, and water. Cover and simmer for 30 minutes, stirring occasionally.

4. Peel and de-vein shrimp. Rinse well. Add shrimp to skillet. Cover and simmer for an additional 10 minutes.

5. Cook spaghetti according to package directions, omitting salt. Drain. Serve shrimp sauce over spaghetti.

Eggplant Pasta

The red bell pepper, eggplant, and black olives make this dish a delightfully beautiful presentation, and the flavor with the crunch of the pine nuts is sure to please!

1. In a large skillet or wok, heat olive oil over medium heat. Add eggplant and garlic. Cover and cook until eggplant is just tender, about 5 minutes, stirring occasionally.

2. Add red bell pepper, mushrooms, oregano, and dried crushed red pepper. Sauté until mushrooms are tender, about 4 minutes.

3. Add wine. Cook until mixture absorbs all the moisture, about 4 minutes.

4. Stir in tomato and black olives. Cook until mixture is just heated through. Transfer sauce to a large bowl.

5. Add pasta and pine nuts. Toss until well combined. Serve immediately with lactose-free cheese, if desired.

Eggplant Truths

Contrary to popular belief and practice, it is usually unnecessary to salt and press the juices from eggplant before cooking it. If an eggplant is firm and fresh, its flavor and consistency will be fine without any advance treatment.

Serves 4

2 tablespoons olive oil
3 cups eggplant, peeled, chopped
6 garlic cloves, minced
1 red bell pepper, cut into strips
6 large mushrooms, sliced
1 teaspoon dried oregano, crumbled
½ teaspoon dried crushed red pepper
⅓ cup dry red wine
1 large tomato, chopped
½ cup chopped pitted black olives
12 ounces freshly cooked penne
¼ cup toasted pine nuts
Shredded lactose-free cheese (optional)

Desserts

chapter sixteen

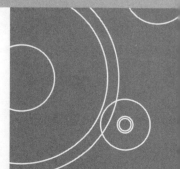

Strawberry Yogurt Scones

Serves 4

Parchment paper
1½ cups all-purpose flour
2½ tablespoons sugar
1 tablespoon baking powder
½ teaspoon baking soda
½ stick margarine
½ cup plain soy yogurt
½ cup fresh coarsely chopped
    strawberries

Try this recipe with other fruits such as fresh blueberries, red raspberries, or peaches.

1. Preheat oven to 350°F. Line bottom of a baking sheet with parchment paper. Set aside.

2. In a medium bowl, combine flour, sugar, baking powder, and baking soda. Add margarine. Blend with a fork until mixture resembles coarse cornmeal.

3. Add yogurt and strawberries. Gently mix to create dough.

4. Pat dough into a 6" circle. Cut into quarters. Place on the parchment-lined baking sheet about an inch apart.

5. Bake scones until tops are golden brown, about 15 minutes. Make sure scones are cooked all the way through.

Baking with Yogurt

In traditional baking you can very quickly learn to substitute soy yogurt in place of milk and buttermilk. The tang of yogurt is a perfect complement to other ingredients such as brown sugars, dried fruits, and molasses, and you'll get feather-light baked goods when you bake with it. Soy yogurt should become a "staple ingredient" in your LI-lifestyle cooking.

Baked Apples

This recipe is an exceptional treat with a dollop of honey-cinnamon yogurt.

1. Preheat oven to 350°F. Spray an 8" × 8" baking dish with nonstick cooking spray. Set aside.

2. Core and thinly slice apples. Toss apples with apple juice in a medium bowl.

3. In a small bowl, combine brown sugar, cornstarch, cinnamon, nutmeg, and salt. Mix well. Sprinkle brown sugar mixture over apples. Stir gently until apples are well coated.

4. Pour apples into prepared baking dish. Bake until sauce is bubbling and the edges of apples begin to brown, about 40 minutes.

5. In a small bowl, combine yogurt, honey, and cinnamon. Stir until well mixed. Divide apples into four dessert dishes and top with yogurt topping.

Serves 4

Nonstick cooking spray
4 Granny Smith apples
¼ cup unsweetened apple juice
¼ cup brown sugar
2 tablespoons cornstarch
½ teaspoon cinnamon
¼ teaspoon nutmeg
¼ teaspoon salt
1 cup plain soy yogurt
1 tablespoon honey
¼ teaspoon cinnamon

Banana Citrus Trifle

Serves 8

8 ounces commercial angel
　food cake
1 tablespoon lime juice
3⅓ cups sliced banana
3 oranges
¼ cup sugar
¼ cup water
1½ teaspoons grated orange
　rind
1½ teaspoons grated lime rind
1½ cups vanilla soy yogurt

A trifle makes a beautiful centerpiece presentation for a special occasion, and this one is a very easy recipe. If presentation isn't what you need, just use a large plastic bowl to make the trifle and dig in!

1. Cut cake into ¼"-thick slices. Set aside. In a medium bowl, pour lime juice over banana slices. Set aside.

2. Peel and section oranges over a small saucepan, reserving juice. Set orange sections aside in a small bowl.

3. Combine sugar and water with orange juice in saucepan. Stir well. Bring to a boil over medium heat. Cook uncovered until mixture is reduced to ⅓ cup, about 5 minutes. Remove from heat. Stir in grated orange and lime rinds.

4. Pour mixture over banana slices. Toss gently, combining well. Arrange half of cake slices in a 2-quart trifle bowl. Spoon half of banana mixture over cake slices. Spread half of the yogurt over banana mixture; then arrange half of orange sections over yogurt.

5. Repeat layering procedure with remaining cake, banana mixture, yogurt, and orange sections. Cover tightly. Chill for at least 6 hours.

Chocolate Brownies

You can make these already healthy brownies a tad healthier by substituting whole wheat pastry flour for some of the all-purpose flour, which will make the texture even smoother!

1. Preheat oven to 350°F. Coat a 9" × 13" baking dish with cooking spray.

2. In a large bowl, combine sugar, flour, cocoa powder, baking powder, baking soda, and salt.

3. In a blender, combine applesauce, tofu, soy milk, and vanilla. Process until well blended.

4. Add tofu mixture to dry ingredients. Mix well. Scrape batter into prepared pan.

5. Bake until top is dry, about 45 minutes. Leave in pan to cool. Cut into bars.

Cocoa Rocks!

There have been many studies linking cocoa and dark chocolate with health benefits. Cocoa and chocolate contain a large amount of antioxidants that may keep high blood pressure down, reducing the risk of heart attack and stroke. The darker chocolate with the most concentrated cocoa proves to be the most beneficial.

Yields 24 brownies

Nonstick cooking spray
2¼ cups granulated sugar
1½ cups all-purpose flour
1½ cups unsweetened cocoa powder
1½ teaspoons baking powder
1½ teaspoons baking soda
½ teaspoon salt
1 cup unsweetened apple-sauce
1 cup soft tofu
¾ cup chocolate soy milk
2 teaspoons vanilla extract

Blueberry Yogurt Crumble

Serves 12

1 cup sugar
2 teaspoons cinnamon
¼ teaspoon nutmeg
2 tablespoons plus 1 stick soy margarine
1½ cups brown sugar
1 egg
1 teaspoon baking soda
2½ cups flour
1 cup plain soy yogurt
1 teaspoon vanilla
½ teaspoon lemon zest
2 cups fresh blueberries (frozen may be substituted)

This lactose-free delight is comparable to old-fashioned blueberry buckle. It's yummy served warm, but it's also tasty as it cools down!

1. Preheat oven to 350°F. Grease and flour a 9" × 13" baking pan.

2. Combine sugar, cinnamon, and nutmeg in a small bowl. Blend 2 tablespoons soy margarine into sugar mixture with a fork. Large crumbs will form.

3. In a medium mixing bowl, cream the stick of soy margarine and brown sugar with an electric mixer. Add egg, mixing well. Stir baking soda into flour in a measuring cup.

4. Reduce mixer speed, adding flour gradually, scraping sides of bowl as necessary. When flour is well blended, add yogurt, vanilla, and lemon zest. Mix well at medium speed for 4 minutes.

5. Pour batter into prepared pan. Sprinkle fresh blueberries over top, pressing them very lightly into batter. Sprinkle crumbly topping across top. Bake for 45 minutes. Cool on a rack. Serve warm.

Chocolate Layer Cake

Cooking with coffee is becoming quite the rage, so here's a recipe with cold coffee. You won't even know the tofu is there; it soaks up the coffee flavor and adds to the smooth texture of this chocolate delight!

1. Preheat oven to 350°F. Grease and flour two 8" round cake pans.

2. In a large bowl, whisk together tofu, syrup, coffee, and vanilla until well blended and smooth. Sift together cocoa powder, flours, baking powder, baking soda, and cinnamon.

3. Add dry ingredients to tofu mixture in mixing bowl. Beat with an electric mixer until smooth, about 3 minutes. Divide batter between cake pans. Bake until cake springs back to touch, about 15 minutes.

4. Cool in pans on wire racks for 10 minutes, then invert cakes onto racks. Cool completely. Frost with Tofu Chocolate Frosting recipe (this chapter).

Serves 12

1 cup puréed firm tofu
1 cup maple syrup
¾ cup brewed strong coffee, cold
2 teaspoons vanilla extract
1 cup unsweetened cocoa powder
¾ cup whole wheat pastry flour
½ cup all-purpose flour
1 teaspoon baking powder
1 teaspoon baking soda
½ teaspoon ground cinnamon
Tofu Chocolate Frosting (Chapter 16)

Tofu Chocolate Frosting

Serves 12

10.5 ounces extra-firm tofu
2 teaspoons vanilla extract
6 ounces dairy-free semisweet
    chocolate, melted
Fresh raspberries for garnish
    (optional)

There's something luxurious about the combination of chocolate with raspberries when the two hit your palate together.

1. Place tofu, vanilla, and chocolate in a blender. Process until smooth.

2. Place one cake layer on a serving plate. Spread with ½ cup frosting.

3. Top with second cake layer. Frost top and sides.

4. Garnish with raspberries, if desired.

Tofu Is a Friendly Ingredient

You're going to find as you experiment with your own recipes in converting them to lactose-free that tofu can "fill in" so many places to provide both the texture and consistency you crave. Don't let tofu intimidate you! Tofu is not only a friendly ingredient but it is very LI-friendly!

Frozen Peanut Butter Pie

This dessert is easy to make and beautiful to serve! The creamy, peanut buttery texture is delicately delightful!

1. Combine all ingredients except pie shell in a blender.

2. Process on medium-high speed until mixture is very smooth and creamy.

3. Pour into prepared pie shell. Freeze overnight.

4. Allow to thaw for about 10 minutes before serving.

Serves 8

1 pound firm tofu, drained
¾ cup peanut butter
½ cup honey
¼ cup oil
1 teaspoon vanilla
½ teaspoon salt
1 graham cracker pie shell

Minty Raspberry Sorbet

Yields 7 servings

2 cups burgundy wine
1 cup water
½ cup sugar
⅓ cup minced fresh mint
1⅓ cups fresh raspberries
2 tablespoons unsweetened
   orange juice
1½ tablespoons lemon juice

Make your own fresh sorbets and you won't ever miss ice cream! Experiment to make your own varieties; the possibilities are endless.

1. Rinse a cheesecloth and squeeze dry. Fold and set aside.

2. In a heavy saucepan, combine wine, water, sugar, and fresh mint. Bring to a boil over medium heat, stirring constantly until sugar is dissolved. Boil for 3 minutes without stirring.

3. Remove from heat. Allow to cool completely. Line a colander with a double layer of cheesecloth, allowing cheesecloth to extend over edge of colander. Place colander in a large bowl.

4. Pour mixture into colander, allowing liquid to drain into bowl. Discard mint. Place raspberries in a blender. Process until smooth. Strain purée. Discard seeds. Add purée, orange juice, and lemon juice to wine mixture. Stir until well mixed.

5. Pour into freezer can of a 2-quart electric freezer. Freeze according to manufacturer's instructions. Scoop sorbet into individual dessert bowls. Serve immediately.

Peachy Tofu Ice Cream

Smooth and fresh, peach ice cream is definitely tasty. You'll be more than pleased with this recipe that allows you to have your ice cream and eat it, too!

1. Peel peaches and chop. Squeeze juice from lemons.

2. In a small bowl combine chopped peaches, fresh lemon juice, and 1 cup sugar. Cover tightly and refrigerate for at least an hour, allowing flavors to mingle.

3. In a large bowl, combine peach mixture with soy milk, tofu, additional sugar, vanilla, and salt.

4. Divide mixture into four equal batches. Process each batch in a blender until consistency is smooth and creamy.

5. Pour into freezer cans of two 4-quart electric freezers. Freeze according to manufacturer's instructions.

Fresh, Ripe Peaches

Not only do fresh, ripe peaches smell like a fruity perfume, they are versatile fruits. Just slicing one for a snack is truly a treat, and there are endless ways to use them in cooking, canning, and freezing! Add to that the high nutritional value—this low-calorie fruit is a rich source of antioxidants, vitamin A, vitamin C, potassium, and fiber.

Yields 26 servings

8 medium peaches
2 lemons
1 cup sugar
3 cups soy milk
1½ pounds soft tofu
1¼ cups sugar
4 tablespoons vanilla
½ teaspoon salt

Cocoa Rice Pudding

Serves 6

½ cup medium-grain white
    rice
10 tablespoons sugar
2 cups rice milk
2 cups coconut milk
1 whole cardamom pod
¼ teaspoon salt
1 teaspoon vanilla extract
⅓ cup cocoa powder
1 tablespoon coconut oil

Coconut milk adds a smooth richness to this rice pudding. Top it with raspberries and eat it for breakfast!

1. In a large saucepan, combine rice, sugar, milks, and cardamom pod; bring to a rolling boil. Reduce heat to very low, cover pan, and simmer for 70–80 minutes, stirring frequently, or until rice is very tender.

2. Remove from heat and stir in salt, vanilla, cocoa powder, and coconut oil; blend well. Remove cardamom pod and pour into bowl; let cool for 30 minutes. Press plastic wrap directly onto pudding surface. Refrigerate until cold.

Sweet Crepes

Crepes are very thin, unleavened pancakes. You can fill these with sorbet, sautéed apples, or another fruit.

1. In a food processor or blender, combine all ingredients except rice milk; process or blend until smooth. Add enough rice milk to make a thin batter. Let stand for 5 minutes.

2. Heat a nonstick 6" skillet over medium heat. Brush with a bit of oil. Using a ½-cup measure, pour about ⅓ cup of the batter into the hot pan. Immediately lift and tilt the pan so the batter coats the bottom. Cook for 2–3 minutes, or until crepe is set and slightly crisp; turn and cook for 30 seconds on second side.

3. As the crepes are finished, place on kitchen towels to cool. Do not stack crepes or they will stick together. You can freeze these, separated by parchment paper or waxed paper, for up to 2 months. To thaw, let stand at room temperature for 20–30 minutes.

Yields 12 crepes

½ cup superfine rice flour
¼ cup brown-rice flour
¼ cup tapioca flour
½ teaspoon xanthan gum
2 tablespoons sugar
⅛ teaspoon salt
¾ cup vegan egg replacer
1 tablespoon vegetable oil
1 teaspoon vanilla
4–6 tablespoons rice or soy milk

Strawberry Sorbet

Yields 4 cups;
Serving size ½ cup

1½ cups water
1 cup sugar, divided
6 cups strawberries
1 tablespoon lemon juice
⅛ teaspoon salt
2 tablespoons vodka, if
   desired

Sorbets are basically sugar, water, and fruit; that's all! The vodka, or other alcohol, gives it a softer texture by keeping it from freezing rock hard.

1. In a heavy saucepan, combine water and ¾ cup sugar and bring to a boil. Simmer over low heat for 7–8 minutes, or until sugar dissolves completely. Remove from heat and let cool.

2. Hull strawberries and slice. Sprinkle with remaining ¼ cup sugar and stir. Let stand for 30–40 minutes, or until sugar dissolves.

3. Combine strawberry mixture, lemon juice, salt, vodka, and ½ cup of the sugar syrup in a food processor; process until smooth. Strain, if desired, to remove seeds. Stir in remaining syrup. Cover and chill until very cold.

4. Freeze in an ice-cream maker according to manufacturer's directions.

Creamy Raspberry Sorbet

For this recipe, you do need an ice-cream maker for best results. This creamy sorbet is rich and delicious.

1. In a heavy saucepan, combine sugar and water and bring to a boil. Boil until sugar dissolves completely, about 1 minute. Remove from heat and let cool completely.

2. In a food processor, combine sugar mixture, coconut milk, fresh and frozen raspberries, salt, and orange juice. Process until smooth. Cover and refrigerate until very cold, about 3–4 hours. Freeze according to your ice-cream maker's instructions.

Serves 6

1 cup sugar
1 cup water
1 cup coconut milk
2 cups fresh raspberries
2 cups frozen raspberries
⅛ teaspoon salt
2 tablespoons orange juice

Grilled Peaches and Mangoes

Serves 4

2 ripe peaches
1 ripe mango
¼ cup honey
¼ cup brown sugar
1 teaspoon cinnamon
⅛ teaspoon salt
2 tablespoons port wine, if
    desired

Grilled fruit is a great treat, not only in sum-mertime, but all year round.

1. Prepare and preheat grill. Peel peaches and cut into slices. Peel mango and cut into slices. Place fruit in the center of a 12" × 18" piece of heavy-duty aluminum foil.

2. In a small bowl, combine remaining ingre-dients. Drizzle over the fruit. Bring the short edges of the foil together and fold over twice, then fold up the other edges, leaving some room for heat expansion.

3. Grill fruit for 10–12 minutes, turning foil packet once during grilling time. Open packet and serve with Cocoa Rice Pudding (this chapter) or frozen sorbet.

Lactose-Free Menus

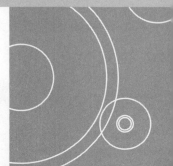

Planning routine family dinners or extravagant celebration meals is a snap with the recipes in this book. Be creative when you plan, and don't be afraid to experiment. Choose recipes with ingredients you like, and substitute ingredients you like for ones you don't. The following are some suggested menus to get you started.

Breakfast Menu	
Breakfast Potatoes	page 16
Bacon Eggs Benedict	page 19
Blueberry Pancakes	page 21
Kiwi Starter	page 40

Dinner Menu 1	
Oriental Spinach Salad	page 88
Oven-Fried Sesame Chicken	page 178
Fried Rice	page 165
Banana Citrus Trifle	page 274

Dinner Menu 2	
Tofu Eggplant Gumbo	page 77
Baked Salmon with Buttered Thyme Potatoes	page 230
Curried Rice	page 254
Cocoa Rice Pudding	page 282

Dinner Menu 3	
Crispy Rice Balls	page 143
Sautéed Yellow Squash and Carrots	page 162
Beef Piccatta	page 202
Grilled Peaches and Mangoes	page 286

Dinner Menu 4	
Greens and Fruit Salad	page 103
Basil Orange Chicken	page 184
Sparkly Carrots	page 168
Baked Apples	page 273

Dinner Menu 5	
Cold Blueberry Soup	page 78
Tofu Tossed Salad	page 90
Poached Salmon	page 232
Strawberry Yogurt Scones	page 272

Dinner Menu 6	
Lentil Soup	page 84
Snapper with Lemon Dill Spinach	page 234
Sautéed Peas	page 158
Peachy Tofu Ice Cream	page 281

Dinner Menu 7	
Tortellini Soup	page 83
Old-Fashioned Meatloaf	page 199
Baked Wild Rice with Herbs	page 253
Minty Raspberry Sorbet	page 280

Dinner Menu 8	
Cool-as-a-Cucumber Salad	page 94
Corn Quesadillas	page 147
Herbed Lamb Chops	page 224
Chocolate Brownies	page 275

Resources

This appendix contains resources to help you explore a lactose-free lifestyle.

National Digestive Diseases Information Clearinghouse

http://digestive.niddk.nih.gov/ddiseases/pubs/lactoseintolerance

The National Digestive Information Diseases Clearinghouse (NDDIC) is a service of the National Institute of Diabetes and Digestive and Kidney Diseases (NIDDK). The NIDDK is part of the National Institutes of Health under the United States Department of Health and Human Services. This website contains a thorough explanation of lactose intolerance in easily understandable terms, complete with figures of the digestive system.

American Dietetic Association

www.eatright.org

The American Dietetic Association's website has information dedicated to educating people about lactose intolerance and nutritional information for children with lactose intolerance.

International Foundation for Functional Gastrointestinal Disorders

www.iffgd.org

The International Foundation for Functional Gastrointestinal Disorders, Inc. (IFFGD) has information on lactose intolerance and other digestive disorders.